SUCCESSFUL
SHARK
FISHING

SUCCESSFUL SHARK FISHING

A. J. CAMPBELL

ILLUSTRATIONS BY CHRIS ARMSTRONG

Ragged Mountain Press
Camden, Maine

International Marine/
Ragged Mountain Press

A Division of The McGraw·Hill Companies

10 9 8 7 6 5 4 3 2 1

Library of Congress Cataloging-in-Publication Data
Campbell, A. J.
    Successful shark fishing / A. J. Campbell ; illustrations by Chris
Armstrong.
        p. cm.
    Includes index.
    ISBN 0-07-009954-5
    1. Shark fishing.   I. Title.
SH691.S4C35   1995
799.1'731—dc20   *95-25818*
                                              CIP

Questions regarding the content of this book should be addressed to:
    Ragged Mountain Press
    P.O. Box 220
    Camden, ME 04843
    207-236-4837

Questions regarding the ordering of this book should be addressed to:
    The McGraw-Hill Companies
    Customer Service Department
    P.O. Box 547
    Blacklick, OH 43004
    Retail customers: 1-800-822-8158
    Bookstores: 1-800-722-4726

A portion of the profits from the sale of each Ragged Mountain Press book is donated to an environmental cause.

Successful Shark Fishing is printed on 60-pound Renew Opaque Vellum, an acid-free paper that contains 50 percent recycled waste paper (preconsumer) and 10 percent postconsumer waste paper.

Historic photos are from the author's private collection. Additional photographs are by the author unless otherwise credited.

    Printed by Quebecor Printing, Fairfield, PA
    Design by Dan Kirchoff
    Production by Dan Kirchoff
    Edited by James R. Babb and Ellen Egan

CONTENTS

FOREWORD

After 20-odd (some of them *really* odd) years of fishing with my good friend A. J. Campbell in the clear yet often turbulent waters of the Gulf of Maine, I have drawn three conclusions: The first is that A. J. has this totally unreasonable "thing" about sharks and shark fishing. The second is that he ranks among the very top handful of shark experts in the Northeast. No question. Third, he sees humor in fishermen and fishing situations where no sane individual would suspect humor could possibly exist. It's a gift, I suppose.

A. J. began fooling around with sharks in the early 1960s, long before they became fashionable. While the rest of us considered blue sharks and the occasional thresher and porbeagle as little more than pests on the bluefin-tuna grounds, A. J. was pioneering specialty light-tackle shark rods and pursuing these critters with fly gear. He experimented with hook styles and leader materials, modified chum buckets, perfected fish-fighting techniques, and unearthed whatever historical lore on shark fishing he could buy, borrow, or sneak out of public libraries under his jacket. And, save for a couple of true trophies, he carefully released all the sharks he caught, a practice that wouldn't gain widespread acceptance for another 15 years.

A. J. has since traveled much of the civilized—and uncivilized—world in pursuit of sharks and other big-game species, and his articles detailing his adventures have appeared in almost every major fishing magazine in the United States. This book, therefore, is a compendium of his experiences at home and abroad, fleshed out with a wealth of information and perspectives provided by a network of shark experts around the globe, seasoned with a pinch of the author's wry Down East humor. *Successful Shark Fishing* may well be the first truly international how-to book on shark angling ever published, and A. J.—along with all those who contributed—can be proud of it.

BARRY GIBSON, EDITOR
SALT WATER SPORTSMAN

PREFACE

I remember my first shark experience as if it were yesterday, although it was back when the "fluid drive" transmission was new. My father had treated me to a day of cod fishing with Captain Bill Eastman out of Seabrook, New Hampshire. It was a beautiful day—calm without a breath of wind—and the cod were large and plentiful.

While waiting for Captain Bill to gaff one of my fish, I watched a big blue shadow appear from beneath the boat. The shark made a slow wondrous circle and chomped my cod, briefly closing its eyes, as if winking and silently proclaiming, "This fish is *mine*, Boy!"

What a wicked fish that shark was—so large and so blue. The next day found me at the Exeter Public Library, pawing through the index. The books I found were by long-dead ichthyologists like Brown and Goode, illustrated with black-and-white line drawings.

But I did identify my shark. It was the Great Blue Whaler, a fish that roamed the temperate oceans, following whaling ships and attacking their grisly carcasses. I checked out the one semimodern book, by Bigelow and Schroeder, took it home, and drew pictures of sharks until my fingers cramped. I was 11 years old.

It would be many years before I actually caught my first rod-and-reel-eating machine, but I'll always remember the one that ate my cod off the Isles of Shoals in 1953. That fish kindled my interest in the toothy clan, and the musty old library books reinforced my hunger to "know."

If you've picked up this book because you want to learn more about fishing for the Ancient Tribe, I hope that it will be an enjoyable and valuable aid. I have tried to include important information for the itinerant sharker as well as the beginner. Besides studying the fish themselves, we'll take a look at the boats, tackle, methods, and even the history of sharking. When you finally apply these tidbits of shark and tackle lore to the waters, I wish you the very best of "greasy" luck.

ACKNOWLEDGMENTS

I thank my wife, Sally, who proofed this manuscript and made helpful suggestions; Jim Babb, who helped with the Big Picture; Curt Garfield, who aided with the British Picture; and Chris Armstrong, who did these excellent line drawings.

This volume would not be possible without the help of the regional shark aficionados who willingly gave their time and expertise. I am grateful to Captains Barry Gibson, Matt Wilder, Cal Robinson, Ben Garfield, Al Ristori, Berle Wilson, and Mike "The Beak" Hurt—all in the United States; Ted Legg of Great Britain; and Rick Pollock of New Zealand. We also thank the following expert international anglers, many of whom are record-holders and also con-tributed photos: in the United States, Wayne McNamee, Rick West, Mark Sosin, John Phillips, Abe Cuanang, and Dave Elm; from the British Isles, Chris Sinclair, Simon Williams, Stan Massey, Rob Richardson, and Chris Bennett; in Australia, Peter Goadby; and from New Zealand, Dr. Mark Feldman. And to Mainers Carl Walsh and Kurt Christensen for excellent shark photos.

A very special thanks goes to Dave Sneath of the Sportfishing Club of the British Isles, who coordinated the remarkable data and photos from Great Britain, and to Derrydale Press, who allowed us to use historical photos from Zane Grey's *Tales of the Angler's Eldorado*.

OUR

Early Avalon guide James Gardner, custom gaff in hand, admires the first known mako caught on rod and reel. Mackerel sharks of this size have made a great comeback in California and sustain a valuable sportfishery.

PRIMEVAL GAMEFISH

Sharks swam the seas long before our ancestors crawled onto land, and today we marvel at the Ancient Tribe—these fish with no bony skeleton, these cold-hearted predators that view almost every living thing as a meal. Ironically, we modern humans have become land sharks, returning to the sea to harvest all that swims or crawls. Today, in certain parts of the globe, the sharks are our only remaining gamefish.

Sharks constitute some of the most diversified families within the finned kingdom; and with more than 350 species to choose from, anglers should have endless possibilities. Most sport-caught fish, however, are from the mackerel- and requiem-shark families. At least another 30 species are taken by anglers, and it's often difficult to distinguish the many subtle differences between members of the tribe. But one thing is certain—all sharks make our hearts race. They are unique among fish.

Compared to bony fishes, which produce high numbers of eggs, female sharks produce very few. All shark fertilization occurs internally, and most species have a long gestation period. Spiny dogfish and basking sharks have the longest gestation periods, at two years and three years, respectively.

All game-status sharks are live-bearers. They usually mate offshore or in southern waters, and their gestation period is so long that the young may be born thousands of miles from their point of conception. As the fish develop within the female, weaker siblings often are eaten prior to birth. Although some species can have as many as 50 pups, most sharks give birth to a far lesser number, often as few as three or four.

During mating, the male approaches the female and swims alongside her, their posterior portions touching. Semen is introduced through a groove in the male's "claspers"; often the male bites the female as "foreplay." A male blue shark may bite the female in several locations during the mating dance. Luckily, the female's skin is much thicker than her mate's.

Several species of sharks, such as the mako, are actually warm blooded. Others swim "in cold blood," neither the quick nor the dead being safe from their bite. All sharks can be aggressive, a trait that can be used to an angler's advantage. Most sharks have poor eyesight: the mako is slightly myopic, while the blue is farsighted.

But sharks have a heightened sense of hearing and an incredibly keen sense of smell. They "hear" with two internal "ear bones," or *otoliths,* and the lateral line, a bundle of vibration-detecting nerve endings just beneath the skin. Sharks are particularly sensitive to low-frequency sounds. Thumping a boat's side or splashing the water will get their attention. Aggressive species—such as porbeagles, threshers, makos, and salmon sharks—are attracted to distress sounds emitted by hooked or injured fish.

A shark's sense of smell is so developed it can detect bleeding prey from great distances. Great whites can smell a dead whale for miles, and they are followed in short order by blues and threshers. The family "sniffer" has developed into a complex organ roughly equal in internal area to the size of a tennis court.

Sharks actively feed at night, although few anglers try for them after sunset. Lights will attract sharks, and we recall the wee hours on Hudson Canyon with the halogens on and a hooked swordfish being followed by a mako and a blue shark.

All sharks have a limited tolerance for temperature variations. They are not found at temperatures below or above their comfort level, and this affects seasonal migration.

Knowledge of the shark's sense of smell, feeding preference, fondness for structure, and temperature limits is key to successful sharking. Let's look at these important areas in detail for the species of interest to anglers.

The Shark's Comfort Zone

Successful shark anglers measure the ocean's surface temperature with an accurate gauge. With the exception of makos, most shark species swim through a wide temperature range, but they have certain preferences:

Species	Range	Comfort Zone
White Shark	50–83°F (10–28°C)	58–75°F (14–24°C)
Mako	59–78°F (15–26°C)	64°F (18°C)
Porbeagle	50–66°F (10–19°C)	52–59°F (11–15°C)
Thresher	54–68°F (12–20°C)	57–64°F (14–18°C)
Blue Shark	51–72°F (11–22°C)	58–65°F (14–18°C)
Tope	52–72°F (11–22°C)	58–66°F (14–19°C)
Tiger Shark	59–85°F (15–29°C)	68–75°F (20–24°C)
Dusky Shark	60–78°F (16–26°C)	65–72°F (18–22°C)
Blacktip	65–86°F (18–30°C)	74–82°F (23–28°C)
Bull Shark	65–85°F (18–29°C)	72–80°F (22–27°C)
Lemon Shark	68–86°F (20–30°C)	76–82°F (24–28°C)
Whitetip	66–86°F (19–30°C)	74–82°F (23–28°C)
Hammerhead	64–86°F (18–30°C)	72–80°F (22–27°C)

The Great Mackerel Sharks

The fast-swimming mackerel sharks comprise a rather small group of active warm-blooded fish with two endearing characteristics—they are tough fighters and excellent eating. A very old family, the mackerel sharks have been traced back to the prehistoric *Carcharodon megalodon* (Greek for "Big as a Burning Camper") from the Pliocene epoch, some 4½ million years ago. The modern group can sustain a body warmth 8 degrees higher than the surrounding sea.

Foremost among mackerel sharks is the invincible **shortfin mako**, respected by tuna and bill fishermen, and historically the sharker's original sport species. The earliest recorded sport-caught mako appears to be Jim Gardner's fish, with Charles Frederick Holder as the probable angler. This "bonito shark" was photographed with Gardner sometime between 1898 and 1908. The cofounder of big-game angling, James Gardner moved to Santa Catalina from England to become one of sportfishing's earliest and most exemplary "boatmen," now more properly referred to as Captain.

Makos, which range the North Atlantic from the Caribbean and Bimini northward to the Gulf of Maine, are intolerant of water much above or below 64°F (18°C). Surface to upper-thermocline sharks, makos supposedly have a sweet tooth for swordfish, which may explain why they taste like them. A mako's diet, listed in the order of preference (for oil content), also includes bluefish, mackerel, squid, school tuna, pogies (menhaden), herring, cod, skipjacks and bonito, and scads.

Mackerel sharks are ovoviviparous, the young developing without a placenta and being nourished by yolk sacks. Usually, the pups resort to cannibalism within the uterus until just one is left. After birth the mako grows faster than most sharks and also digests food more quickly. It can be distinguished from other mackerel sharks by its blue color, abruptly turning to white on the belly, and its "snaggle" teeth, lacking *cusps* (mini-teeth) at their base.

Mako sharks can leap to a height twice their body length and make successive jumps in an amazing show of strength like no other fish. The largest Atlantic makos are concentrated in the American Northeast. In the Gulf of Maine, we have seen fish that easily exceed 1,000 pounds. One mako, estimated at 1,200 pounds and hooked on a 4/0 outfit, never even knew it was attached to a line, and took our client down to the spool arbor. Large makos also frequent the Indian Ocean, and the 1,115-pound, International Game Fish Association all-tackle mako comes from the isle of Mauritius, off the southeast coast of Africa.

The mako of the Pacific, formerly called a **bonito shark,** can range from California to Chile and on out to the Indo-Pacific, especially off the coasts of New Zealand and Australia. An active shark of the open ocean, it dines on school tunas, bonito, mackerel, sardines, and anchovies. Virtually all modern anglers, from California to New Zealand, call the bonito shark a mako. Whether the two fish are actually different species is an argument for taxonomists. But we're anglers, so from this point on, a mako is a mako!

3

Some makos jump higher than others. With a tremendous bulk, this near-grander is coming back down for a crash landing. (It broke off, proving that even with heavy tackle, it pays to bow to the fish.)

The North Atlantic **porbeagle** is very similar to the mako and easily confused with its larger cousin. The porbeagle has similar teeth but with a pair of cusps at their base. Cobalt blue like makos, porbeagles often have a distinctive white area at the posterior base of the primary dorsal. Porbeagles also have a chunky body with a secondary "keel" just before the tail. They prefer cold water, in the low to mid-50s (11–15°C), and have been caught in the Gulf of Maine and off England's Cornwall shores as early as May and as late as December. The largest individuals are taken from Scotland's North Coast between November and March.

Whether mackerel, herring, or small cod, they like their meals wiggling, and dead baits are often ignored. Porbeagles, reaching weights of 400 pounds, often move into coastal waters in pursuit of mackerel.

The rare Pacific **salmon shark** is the equivalent of the North Atlantic's porbeagle, and may even be the same species. It ranges from San Diego to Alaska, following the salmon and herring. Adults are stout like the porbeagle but, unlike the eastern version, have dark blotches on their lower body and can exceed 500 pounds. We have no recent records of sport catches of this very edible fish, and it would be a great coup for an angler to land one.

The largest mackerel shark, the **great white**, is the most dangerous animal in the ocean. Although found in every temperate sea, they remain uncommon. Compared to other mackerel sharks, whites have larger, serrated teeth and a gray or brownish upper body. On occasion, a great

white will leap clear of the water when hooked. Most world records for this fish were taken in the 1950s by Queensland's Mr. and Mrs. Bob Dyer. Today we suggest that great whites be released, although anglers vying for membership in the IGFA's Thousand Pound Club will continue to pursue this fish as the Ultimate Shark.

The great white prefers warm meals, and California has closed all fishing for great whites to save the species for its purpose in life: eating sea lions, whose populations are beginning to exceed the carrying capacity of local ecosystems. The great white ventures close to land in search of gourmet fare. Two great whites harpooned

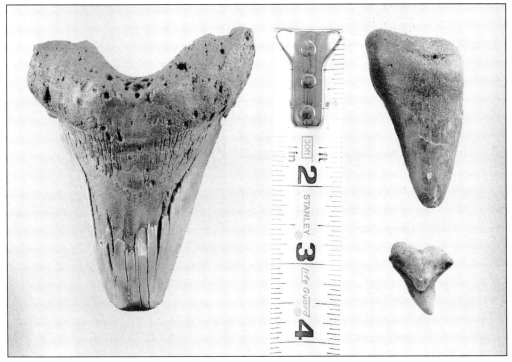

Fossil sharks can be judged only by their teeth. Carcharodon megalodon *(left) was 40 feet long. The white shark and big thresher (top and lower right) are still active big game.*

during the 1950s in Maine's Penobscot Bay had been feeding on harbor seals in the rocky shallows.

Requiem Sharks

In a species count, the requiem family ranks high. Most abundant of the requiems, the popular **blue shark** has a wide temperature tolerance and ranges the globe. In the western Atlantic, blues migrate from the Caribbean to the Gulf of Maine. An intermixing eastern Atlantic population migrates from South Africa to the British Isles.

Blue sharks are pelagic and migrate in unisex packs. Females that have mated at least once will have the characteristic bite marks caused by the male. When blue sharks are found in numbers, a boat can release as many as a dozen fish in an outing. Blues feed upon a wide variety of lesser fish: herring, cod, mackerel, and shad. Although known carrion eaters, they can be fussy at times.

The great blues can grow to a length of 13 feet and weigh up to 450 pounds. They are "light for their weight," as Captain Barry Smith says, and have long pectoral fins and a long upper tail lobe. Popular light-tackle game, average blues can be taken on fly, casting, and spinning outfits. The largest specimens are found in the Gulf of Maine and off Australia.

The "blue whaler" is replaced in tropical waters by the **oceanic whitetip**, a shark of similar length and stouter body. Whitetips prefer the deep (100 fathoms or more) but congregate along the edges of barrier reefs. Ranging along the western

Many large requiems have a nictitating membrane, or third eyelid. Triggered when the fish opens its mouth or strikes an object, the membrane slips up over the eye. Use this reflex "wink" as a visual guide for setting the hook on a baited blue shark or tiger.

Atlantic and the eastern Pacific out to Hawaii, these fish have recently been targeted by anglers.

Like blue sharks, oceanic whitetips often travel in packs and are readily identified by the adult's white-tipped fins. Although a common shark, the species' first all-tackle record—a 146-pound fish taken by Pamela Basco off Kona, Hawaii—wasn't registered with the IGFA until 1992.

Some requiem sharks are found inshore, and **brown** (**sandbar**) and **dusky** sharks often enter bays and rivermouths. The lead gray dusky can grow to more than 500 pounds, but typical catches are much smaller. Another denizen of the open ocean, the dusky ranges south to Brazil. The little brown shark is more of an inshore fish and, since it grows to only about 6 feet, is an excellent light-tackle fighter. Found from southern New England to Brazil, it is common in the Gulf of Mexico.

Off New Jersey, large male browns are usually found in deeper waters, but the females enter bays to give birth to their pups. Both species have a distinct ridge between their first and second dorsal fins, and prefer benthic fare, including sea robins, skates, and flounder.

In the Pacific, the coastal **soupfin shark** mirrors the size and habits of the brown, seldom exceeding 100 pounds. This active requiem jumps and fights well. Characterized by a pointed snout and concave head, this shark will also visit the deep. Soupfins, once heavily targeted by commercials, are common from British Columbia to southern California.

The **tiger shark** reigns as largest of the subtropical requiems, attaining a weight of a ton, with many adults exceeding the "grander" mark. It is occasionally found in shallow water, which is often the pupping ground for gravid females. As its name implies, the tiger is marked with vertical bars that fade as it gets older. In the Atlantic, tigers venture northward to New Jersey but are more abundant in warmer waters.

Most adult tigers are too large for light- or medium-tackle angling. One of the earliest sport-caught tiger sharks, a 1,036-pounder, was taken by Zane Grey off Sydney Head, Australia. Like the great white, the tiger is a heavy-tackle fish, sought after by members of the Grander Club; and the largest modern specimens are taken year-round from New South Wales.

Spinner (**greater blacktip**) and **blacktip sharks** are exciting requiem sharks for the flats fisherman. The spinner can grow to 8 feet; but most individuals are smaller and appropriate for light tackle. They are numerous from the Florida Flats to Puerto Rico, and are considered high game; the blacktip and spinner are noted for twisting leaps when hooked in deeper water. Both fish have a longer snout than the bull shark, and the blacktip has larger eyes than the spinner.

Another popular flats species, the **lemon shark**, can reach 11 feet, but most of the flats crowd are less than half that length. Lemons are readily available to light-tackle anglers. Like the blacktips and spinners, they are common throughout the Gulf of Mexico, south to Panama. All three species eat small baitfish and rays, as well as most crustaceans.

The **bull shark** has a wider range than the blacktip. Bull sharks have been caught from Hatteras to Panama and can be found in shallow waters throughout most of the tropics, cruising inlets and ascending river systems into fresh water. We have seen 8-foot bulls entering the Rio San Juan in Nicaragua, where they continue up to the lake of the same name. A tad sluggish, they won't take a fly or crankbait but will hit natural baits with relish, although they'll eat them plain too. In fact, these fish have been known to attack bathers and are considered the most dangerous of the requiem sharks.

The **tope** is a most sought-after member of the family, occurring in the eastern North Atlantic and the South Pacific. This shallow-water shark is a lively gamefish of England and

Wales, but the majority of record tope come from the waters of Parengarenga Harbor, New Zealand.

No matter where it's found, the benthic-feeding tope seldom exceeds 70

Mako

Mackerel

Porbeagle

Thermocline

Since different species of sharks often seek different areas of the water column, the placement of your baits—near the surface, above the thermocline, or near bottom—may determine which species you attract.

Tope

Leopard

pounds; most run 20 to 40 pounds. Touted as much better fighters than blue sharks, tope are popular in temperate light-tackle circles; although they're good eating, most are released.

Members of the requiem family can truly offer the Mass of the Dead: wire-men and gaffers should watch for the telltale arc followed by a nasty set of teeth. The two most dangerous species are the bull and

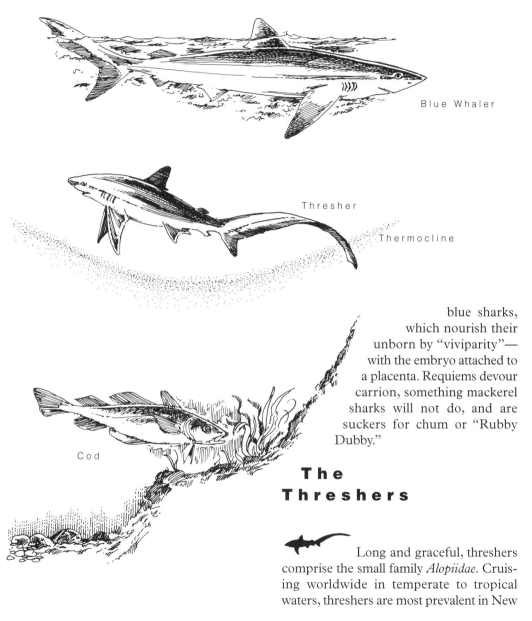

Blue Whaler

Thresher

Thermocline

Cod

blue sharks, which nourish their unborn by "viviparity"— with the embryo attached to a placenta. Requiems devour carrion, something mackerel sharks will not do, and are suckers for chum or "Rubby Dubby."

The Threshers

Long and graceful, threshers comprise the small family *Alopiidae*. Cruising worldwide in temperate to tropical waters, threshers are most prevalent in New

Worldwide, threshers are among our greatest toothy game. Attacking trolled or chummed baits, they use their tail as a lethal weapon.

England during the summer; in California year-round; and off the coasts of New Zealand, where they may attain their largest size, during the warmer months. Usually found offshore, thresher packs swim around a school of baitfish and herd them with their well-muscled tails, which are as long as their bodies. Individuals are frequently taken by trolling, and the tail is often foul-hooked when the thresher slaps the bait to stun it.

The thresher is a strong adversary, often jumps, and is very good eating, comparable to mako and swordfish. It can reach a length of 20 feet and a weight of 1,000 pounds, although most sport-caught individuals are far smaller. Even smaller threshers are great fighters, ranking with makos in the California sportfishery.

Bigeye threshers are uncommon cousins of the thresher. They are sometimes caught on the surface by chumming; but as their peepers proclaim, they are pelagics that prefer the depths. Most threshers have grayish to dark charcoal backs, abruptly breaking to white undersides. They prefer "chopper" bluefish, squid, mackerel, herring, and needlefish.

Wicked-Odd Hammerheads

The family *Sphyrnidae* has a curiously odd-looking membership, including the four species of

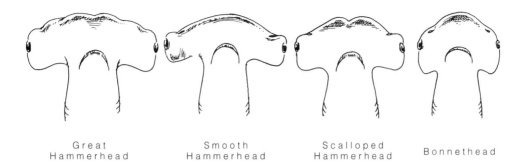

Great Hammerhead   Smooth Hammerhead   Scalloped Hammerhead   Bonnethead

hammerheads. Like a few of the requiem sharks, they are viviparous, with the unborn pups attached to an umbilical cord. The **great hammerhead** can grow to 18 feet. This seldom-caught, warm bluewater species ranges from Cape Hatteras to South America and is most common in Florida waters. Hammerheads fight fairly well, perhaps due to their great size, and can be taken on medium and heavy tackle.

The **smooth hammerhead** often comes inshore, with gregarious schools migrating along the beaches of Florida. We have seen them chasing mullet to within the surf line at Juno Beach. Ranging throughout the tropics, this prolific species runs up to 14 feet. The frontal head area is slightly and smoothly curved, and its teeth are also smooth. Smooth hammerheads are also plentiful in the Indo-Pacific and are caught in Australia and New Zealand.

Next in size and abundance, is the **scalloped hammerhead**, which grows to 12 feet. Encountered as far north as south Jersey, most scalloped hammerheads are found in subtropical and tropical waters of both the Atlantic and eastern Pacific; they are caught regularly in the Gulf of Mexico. The scalloped hammerhead has smooth teeth, and the corners of its mouth extend below the rear of its head, which has a

more anterior curve than the smooth hammerhead's.

The smallest of the family, the **bonnethead shark,** seldom exceeds 3 feet. It ranges worldwide in tropical seas, but unlike most hammerheads, it will enter the flats to feed. Tropical flats are also the bonnethead's rearing ground, and these small fish can be taken on flies and ultralight tackle. The frontal portion of the head has more curve than do the heads of all other members of the family. All hammerheads have a particular fancy for stingrays, and will also eat shrimp and crabs as well as inshore baitfish.

Lesser Game Species

 **Six-** and **sevengill sharks** are living primitive fossils found—but seldom caught—in deep Atlantic waters. These odd-looking sharks are common in the temperate Pacific, especially in northern California waters. Both species can grow large, and are distinguished from all other sharks by their single dorsal fin. Bottom feeders by nature, they are frequently taken by small-craft and headboat anglers in San Francisco Bay.

Among the many other sharks that are good eating but not great gamefish are the **spiny** and **smooth dogfish**—those small Atlantic dolts that "fight" only when snagged on trout gear, and often show up to chew on baits meant for "real" sharks. Smooth doggies are found below the range of their spiny brethren, and are common from southern New England to Uruguay. All doggies are reasonably good eating, most often served in English fish 'n' chips.

Pacific bottom fishermen often catch the handsome **leopard sharks,** which are sometimes classed in the requiem family—taxonomists do not agree on what the leopard shark is or on whether it is a requiem. The females attain a maximum length of 5 feet. These active fish range from Oregon to Baja. A primitive cousin living within the same geographical area, the bull-headed **horned shark,** is also mottled but is not quite as colorful; it has a spine at the base of each dorsal fin. Both species are fun on light tackle and are good eating.

Sand sharks, sometimes called sand tigers, are common inshore species of the ground shark family. Ground sharks can grow to 10 feet; they eat butterfish, bluefish, menhaden, and small benthic fish. They are occasional visitors to the Gulf of Maine, and their range extends to the Gulf of Mexico. In the Pacific, sand tigers have been taken in California and out to Tahiti. Due to their bulk, they will put up a decent, albeit slow, fight. They are easy to identify, with large dorsal fins of equal size.

The shallow-water **nurse shark** has more southerly quarters. It reaches 14 feet, fights in slow motion, and eats benthic fish, shrimp, and crabs. This was the fish that shredded humans unmercifully in the terrible B-movie *Mako—Jaws of Death*.

Basking sharks are much too large to catch even if one could hook them; they are pelagic plankton feeders and will not take bait. Often seen on offshore North Atlantic shark grounds, basking sharks are good indicators of "tack" mackerel and the sport sharks that chase them. Surprisingly, these fish are the closest relatives of the mackerel sharks, and have similar fin structure. Because of the similarity, smaller basking sharks are sometimes mistakenly harpooned.

Even larger than the basker, the **whale shark** can reach 60 feet, and is a good indicator of areas with a healthy food chain. These giants are impressive fish, exceeded in size only by the whales. Unfortunately, the population of both species is dwindling; by some estimates, only 400 basking sharks remain, worldwide.

Sharks in Trouble

We are fortunate to have a few sharks that can rip line with the best of saltwater gamefish. The mackerel shark, thresher, tope, blue shark, lemon, and blacktips are great sport on appropriate tackle, burning fond memories into the hearts of anglers who hook them.

But sharks that fight well, are popular,

Abe Cuanang

Handsomely attired in a silver gray suit with black overlays, the leopard shark is not only striking in appearance, but also a very game fighter for its size.

or make excellent table fare, dwindle in numbers every year. Since *Jaws*, the American imagination has waded blood-red through the sharking experience. A number of shark tournaments, from Montauk to the New Jersey shore, initiated destructive annual blue shark kills. The uremic carcasses dragged to the weigh-in were not a pretty sight.

Enlightened anglers learned that the blue shark takes up to 8 years to become sexually mature, lives for maybe 40 years, and is irreplaceable in the ocean niche it occupies. We hope that the shark sideshows, like kill billfish tournaments, will soon be retired to history. Meanwhile, it's up to concerned anglers to lead the way to more sensible treatment of sharks.

We can't point a finger without glancing at photos from angling's past, however. From the emergent "big game" sportfishery of the 1930s until the release ethic of the 1970s, inedible requiem sharks (and a lot of other fish) were slapped onto "sportfishing" docks worldwide as trophies of the hunt. This waste, even spread over 50 years, does not equal the number of inedible sharks destroyed annually by the commercial sector. Today, anglers release fish humanely if they are not gourmet fare, and many are tagged for science.

Edible sharks have more of a story. The deplorable commercial practice of *finning* (the removal of all the fins of living sharks for the Asian soup cartel) has finally

Mike "The Beak" Hurt

Anglers are encouraged to return sharks to their domain. This young California mako was tagged and released by Captain Mike "The Beak" Hurt.

been outlawed. Yet longliners target sharks with new vigor, as the stocks of other large edible fish decline from overharvesting. The ongoing worldwide collapse of the commercial finfish industry will not be kind to sharks, and edible species will receive stock-breaking pressure. At the same time, sharks of no commercial value will be decimated as bycatch, as the netters and longliners try frantically to fill quotas in the shortest period of time.

Even the shark's food is threatened. As groundfish stocks dwindle, commercial fishermen look for new species to tap. The often obtuse National Marine Fisheries Service encourages the harvest of "under-utilized" species, citing the Atlantic mackerel stocks as prime for picking. In Maine, the state authorities have made an ongoing deal with the Ukrainians, selling off the menhaden and herring stocks to the strains of a distant balalaika. The rampant removal of mackerel, menhaden, and herring from the biomass will drastically reduce the natural food supply of all larger predators, including sharks, tuna, and billfish. This dicking with the ocean's food chain by both federal and state governments could prove catastrophic.

The prognosis is not good for the world's shark population. Historically, sharks have had little commercial or angling value, but they are becoming increasingly—and alarmingly—popular, both as food and as sportfish. In 1993, the National Marine Fisheries Service instituted its tardy Shark Conservation Program, finally setting limits on the commercial sector as well as on the sportfishery.

The NMFS action is welcomed since shark stocks will only rebound when tighter restrictions are imposed. All of us use this resource as dinner fare, and some of us occasionally keep fish for records, so we can't condemn anyone else for doing likewise. But through good conservation practices, the tide of dwindling numbers can be turned. We hope to experience the power, wonder, and grace of these amazing animals for generations to come.

2 SHARKING

Jim Hinkley's 685-pound mako was taken in the Gulf of Maine from a 25-foot boat. Midsize craft are good sharking platforms, offering stability and range.

Carl Walsh

OFFSHORE AND ON

We have taken a broad look at some great angling potential—these mackerel, requiem, and thresher sharks. Now let's learn where to find them and how to catch them. Pelagic species necessitate able craft that can run offshore, while shallow-water members of the tribe can be taken from skiffs, from the beach, and by wading. Whether we fish from a boat or from shore, successful sharking hinges on learning when the various species migrate through your local area, where to find them, and what signs to look for.

When to Find Sharks

Like many other large fish, sharks roam the oceans along timeless migration routes. Migration patterns for the most popular species have been revealed by the many shark-tagging programs, some of which have been around for almost three decades. The governing factor in all shark migrations seems to be water temperature; the fish follow specific comfort zones to remain in their own eternal summer.

Makos have the shortest migration routes. The western-Atlantic population rarely crosses the Mid-Atlantic Ridge into the eastern Atlantic, and the Indo-Pacific fish do not seem to move over to the eastern areas, apparently due to the cold-water barriers between zones. For the same reason, two separate populations of tope occupy regions at opposite ends of the globe. Blue sharks, however, can traverse colder regions and may intermix worldwide. The high- and low-temperature limits of each species of shark determine just how far the fish will travel.

Throughout the globe, sharks appear in their seasonal migration as the local waters warm. A savvy sharker will listen to marine weather broadcasts to keep abreast of increasing surface temperatures, preparing boat and tackle for the approaching season. Often, the water temperature close to shore may be cooler than farther out in deeper zones. We have traveled over miles of 50-odd-degree water before hitting the warmer 60-plus-degree currents that hold our ultimate prize.

Continuing their migration, sharks

will move on when waters get too warm for comfort. The makos, which appear to winter from the Carolinas to the Bahamas, travel northward in late spring, passing by the Outer Banks and arriving at the Jersey-Metro region in June. When warming waters exceed their comfort level, the makos continue up to Cape Cod and the Gulf of Maine. We are firm believers in fishing correct water temperature. To a great degree, successful sharking can be attributed to an understanding of temperature requirements.

In the Company of Sharks

Other indicators of prime shark territory are heavy concentrations of bait, birds, sea lions, seals, and other large fish. "Life draws life," as Captain Mike "The Beak" Hurt once said. Where water temperatures are suitable, look for an abundance of life.

Throughout the oceans, birds work over baitfish and the leavings of larger predators. Most common are various gulls and terns, which dive and hit the surface when they're active. Sometimes, after a feeding spree by larger fish, the birds rest on the water or floating debris until the next flurry of marine activity. Chick birds, or petrels as they are more commonly called, will raft in numbers, waiting in anticipation.

Many birds appear as a few individuals, winging their way close to the ocean's surface as they look for leavings. Gannets and boobies (often called *gaviotas* in the tropics) and shearwaters tend to fly low to the water and can go undetected if anglers are looking skyward. During a chum drift, shearwaters often dive, swimming deep enough to steal sharkers' bait. The great cir-cling man-o-war or frigate birds hover directly over larger fish, and we always welcome their keen eyesight.

Concentrations of small surface baitfish—sardines, anchovies, mackerel, menhaden, and herring—all support the big brutes that feed upon them. What a thrill to see bait showering as a thresher raids their schooling world. Anglers should also use their depthsounders to look deep for schools of benthic fare, such as cod and whiting. Depth machines will tip sharkers off to mid-depth schools of bonito, tunny, and scads. Wherever baitfish are abundant, sharks are close at hand.

Often sharks are spotted as they fin along the surface, with just their first dorsal and caudal fins above the water. The most active and sporting species will sometimes "free jump."

The presence of other large fish will tip us off to shark populations. Tuna are foremost indicators of warmer waters and an abundance of bait, and porpoise will hang with the tuna. Giant basking sharks and whales follow the krill and plankton pushed by upwellings to the ocean's surface. All smaller mackerel, herring, sardines, and menhaden feed upon these minute crustaceans.

Pelagic and Coastal Locations

The food chain runs from the tiniest copepods to the largest predators, whether in the deep or in the surf line. Like other offshore game, pelagic sharks are plentiful in areas with a high concentration of baitfish. For instance, an area heavy in cod, herring, and mackerel will support members of the upper end of the food chain—tuna, sword-

When sharking, scan the surface for the finning fish. Basking and mackerel sharks often show just their dorsal fins. This basker indicates a high plankton area, often rich in tack mackerel and the sharks that feed upon them.

fish, and sharks. Almost always, the highest biomass occurs over structure. In the north-eastern United States and the eastern Pacific, this shapes into underwater mounts. (Two-thirds of the world's peaks are under the ocean.) In the tropical Atlantic, structure is defined as reefs and wrecks. Often, the best sharking will be found when a boat's chum line sinks over broken bottom at an ideal temperature. Deep structure, in more than 20 fathoms of water, will often hold makos, blue sharks, and threshers—the pelagic species. Great whites and porbeagles will enter coastal areas containing shallow reefs.

Sea conditions are also a factor in sharking success. Thermal temperature breaks, vertically above or below a thermo-cline, or tidal and current breaks at the sur-face are worth investigating. Many pelagics will follow "temperature lines" in areas of depth but little structure, such as off the Carolinas and Florida.

Although they may also indicate tem-perature breaks, weed lines often denote current breaks and often conceal a myriad of baitfish. Sharks, pelagic and coastal, will be found along weed lines—rockweed in the north and sargasso in the tropical Atlantic—as well as around kelp paddies in the Pacific. The largest school of sharks we have ever seen, 25 to 30 lemons, was tight against a weed line that separated the brown and blue water off the Rio Colorado.

Sharks will hold along drop-offs and channels in shallower water. Outside edges along river inlets and sandbars will attract many requiem species: the sandbar sharks, duskies, lemons, bulls, and blacktips. Hammerheads are noted for cruising in both deep and shallow waters.

Initially, finding sharks may not be easy. Often we have gone to good locations with perfect structure and temperatures only to find them void of the sharks that were there the day before. Even experts can miss once in a while, and that brings us to the last tip on finding sharks: Ask an old sharker about local areas. Each port and seacoast area has one or two old-timers who have run into sharks. Whether commercial or sporting, seasoned fishermen have a wealth of information they are often willing to share.

Shark-Fishing Craft

Shark anglers can use a wide variety of boats, from the simplest skiff to the tournament-rigged sportfisherman. To get to blue-water species, a boat must be seaworthy but not necessarily large.

When we first started sharking, the late Captain Bob Colburn and I fished from a 17-foot Mako, and during calm seas it was an adequate platform. We listened to the weather reports well in advance, tried to pick the bluebird days, and enjoyed some exciting Maine sport.

The deepwater shark angler could conceivably encounter trouble aboard such a small craft, however. On one occasion, while being towed through the fog by a large shark, we met up with the *Prince of Fundy*, the giant Portland to Yarmouth ferry, which passed by a little too close.

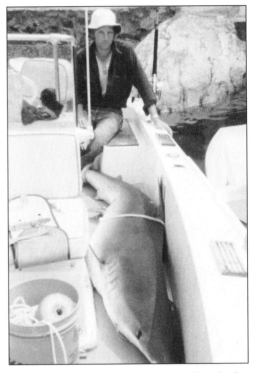

The late Bob Colburn with the large blue shark that took us for a ride. Small craft like this 17-foot Mako are able inshore boats.

Today, a bit wiser and more conservative, we look back at some of our early trips as hair-raising events.

Inshore, the same boat can be put to good duty. In the outer harbors of New Jersey, where small brown sharks are abundant, the little Mako 17- or 19-footer would be ideal. Other shallow-V-hulled models in this class, such as Robalos or Aqua Sports, are excellent platforms.

The Flats Skiff

Similar small craft certainly have their place upon the flats as well, and a shallow-draft fiberglass skiff proves invaluable. Such models as the Hewes Bonefisher and the Dolphin Super Skiff are ideal stalkers in waters where a pushpole is necessary. The average flats skiff is 18 to 20 feet long, is usually powered by a gutsy outboard, and must be light enough to be poled for long periods of time.

Most flats skiffs have a poling platform mounted over the outboard engine. Standing on the platform raises an angler's eye level to about 8 feet above the water's surface, giving a better angle to spot tailing and cruising fish. Skiff pushers try to pole with the wind and sun at their backs or off to either quarter. This gives them the best shot at seeing sharks and allows a fly-rodder to make a good presentation. Since most shark fishing upon the flats is a sight game, tons

of electronics may not be necessary. We consider a VHF radio essential on waters anywhere; if the skiff is to be used for wreck fishing, more gadgets will be needed.

Mighty Midsize Craft

For chumming up sharks around tropical wrecks, a center-console or walk-around Boston Whaler or Grady-White–style boat in the 23- to 25-foot range is ideal. In northern climes, such craft can fish the shark grounds out to 20 miles from port, with sufficient fuel capacity and an experienced operator.

Although we've seen 25-footers on

Hewes

A shallow-draft skiff, such as the Hewes 20-foot Light Tackle is an ideal flats boat. Notice that the poler has kept the sun at his back. This cuts down on glare, making it easier to see tailing sharks.

Like many midsize boats, the Cobia 234 SF has a center console that allows total free-dom for the angler once a shark is hooked up. This 23-footer sports twin outboards for added safety and the high freeboard required for stand-up sharking.

the offshore grounds in the Gulf of Maine and on Hudson Canyon, we would not want to be aboard if the weather turned snotty. A little good sense goes a long way in avoiding trouble. Most boats in this category can hang dual outboards or a single large outboard backed by a smaller trolling motor.

Although a midsize craft allows anglers to fish for deepwater sharks in relative safety and comfort, if it will be used for makos, we suggest choosing the fish very carefully, putting discretion over machismo. Recently a Grady-White owner fishing a deepwater bank in the Gulf of Maine saw a 14-foot mako coming up his chum slick. He wisely reeled in his offerings, started his engine, and found another spot.

The Bluewater Sportfisherman

Offshore craft in the 28- to 36-foot league are well suited to waters that can turn into maelstroms in no time flat. Anglers gunning for the really big brutes can't beat a rugged fiberglass sportfisherman in this class. With an abundance of used models on the market, shark anglers find it easier than ever to move up to bigger ones.

There are several advantages to larger, previously owned craft. By the three-year-old stage, boats in this class have the bugs worked out. They also come with amenities for full-day and overnight trips, when it's mighty handy to have a head, a

Walker Agency

*Heading for the shark grounds, a Pursuit 3000 Offshore offers comfort and range.
Similar to many inboards of the 30-foot class, it has a 250-gallon fuel capacity
and an excellent working cockpit.*

galley, and V-berths. And many used boats have a full complement of fishing goodies.

Older wooden craft with brittle fastenings and cracked frames are not ideal deepwater sharking platforms. There is little doubt that such antique craft could split at the seams if thumped by a big mackerel shark. While fishing in a vintage 32-foot Pacemaker, Captain Matt Wilder and I watched a monster "grander" mako pass slowly by our beam while we were chumming. After the fish swam off into our slick, the skipper walked over and muttered, "It's time for a new boat." The next season, we were fishing in the *Lucky Star II,* a rugged 35-foot Bertram.

If you plan on battling a tiger, great white, or giant mako like the one we saw, a **fighting chair** is a virtual necessity. These outsized fish require tackle too heavy for stand-up angling, and the chair coupled with a bucket harness may be the only recourse in landing such trophies. Chair anglers strapped into a bucket use their legs for pumping the rod, and the harness slides fore and aft as the fish is fought. To help the harness slide easily, it may be necessary to lube the chair seat with liquid detergent.

Any fighting chair should be securely through-mounted in the cockpit, either to a large plate mounted under a rugged cockpit sole or to the keel stringer. The chair's gimbal must be strong, and at least one style allows the use of rods built with straight or curved butts. Most sharkers will never have to "sit" on a fish, but many sportfishing boats have a chair for the occasion when it's really needed.

Offshore sportfishermen, usually powered by twin gas or diesel engines, have a greater operating range than their smaller cousins. Most of these craft carry at least 300 gallons of fuel, so sharkers can venture to the outer banks, fish for the day, and not worry about getting back to the dock on fumes. Twin engines are safer too—if one fails, the skipper can still head for the barn without calling for assistance.

Some larger sportfishing boats are designed with a single diesel engine; these cost less to operate than twin-engine craft but entail a small sacrifice in maneuverability. Captain Barry Gibson's new *Shark IV*, designed for a single engine, also has a bow thruster for ease in docking. Single-engine boats do not back down well, though, and track to port or starboard in reverse.

Cockpit Layout

A shark boat's cockpit should have enough room for an angler to move about freely during hookup. There is nothing worse than stumbling around nonessential coolers, line baskets, deck chairs, and other obstructions that seem placed specifically to slam shins. Keep the cockpit sole clean of gurry and paraphernalia, and the enjoyment quotient rises.

If the cockpit has a chair and the angler is fishing stand-up style, the chair's footrest should be removed and stowed below decks. We have slammed our shins into a number of expensive, quality footrests, and can report that "Stand-up, Falldown" angling is not fun. Often, boats have a line attached to a stern cleat and hanging down to the deck, apparently to trip anglers fighting a nice shark. Boatowners should

put these errant lines in the same dark place they can put their footrests.

Boat Handling

As many sharks are landed through proper boat handling as by an angler's skill; successful sharking depends on a savvy, observant helmsperson. Throughout the battle, the skipper keeps the boat just ahead and off to one side of the hooked shark, leading the fish and taking charge. In Australia, where sharks often exceed a grand, boat handlers actually lead the hooked fish by constantly circling it. On large makos in the northeastern United States, we do likewise, although our boat handlers tend to make a wider, sometimes almost imperceptible circle around the hooked set of jaws. The circling technique is the only sure-fire method of keeping the angler's fragile monofilament or Dacron line from touching the shark's sandpaper skin.

Sometimes large sharks will sound deep after hooking, and the angler faces a vertical slugfest, with the advantage in the fish's corner. A knowledgeable skipper will move the boat ahead when this happens, peeling line from the angler's reel. Even though some line has been lost, the judicious boat handler has increased the angle from the rod to the fish so that the shark can be planed toward the surface from this fresh position. This avoids considerable strain on the angler and the tackle.

With extremely light tackle, the boat handler might have to back down immediately on a shark that's stripping a small-capacity reel. Backing down has its good points, but it can load a boat with gallons of seawater as well. Small craft with low-cut outboard motor wells have sunk during such maneuvers. A few years back, the author was dropped aboard a Rampage 28

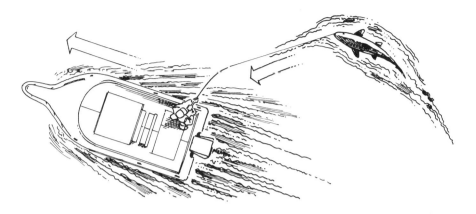

Avoid a potential roll up by leading sharks with the boat. Always fight a shark aft of the stern quarter of the cockpit, and then wire it from this same location.

with a skeleton crew—just an angler and skipper—who needed a wire-man. The boat handler was following a very large fish, perhaps 700 or 800 pounds, constantly backing down until he noticed that the boat was getting logy. Upon cracking a hatch, we discovered gallons of seawater in the bilge—more than the pumps could handle.

The boat handler changed tactics, swung around to point the bow in the fish's direction, and ran on it until we had it off the rear quarter—the preferred method of chasing an outsized fish. On that day, the angler's line "sea-sawed" across boat rod

Several GPS units, such as the new Magellan series, should interest sharkers. These can be interfaced with a ChartMate.

guides so many times that it finally burned and parted. Proper and expedient boat handling could have paid off big-time: aspiring skippers need to take charge; lead the fish, not follow it; and take extra care when the shark gets to leader-grabbing range.

An Electronic and Positioning Advantage

Any sharker after offshore fish should have a bank of accurate and **up-to-date navigational charts** within easy reach. Charts are the ultimate backup if the electronics should go on the fritz. Well-chosen charts of a local area, including all waters fished upon, can get anglers back to shore if they have **a magnetic compass, dividers, parallel rules,** and a knowledge of **dead reckoning.**

A good working **Loran-C** and/or a **GPS** (Global Positioning System) are valuable navigational aids that enable boaters to go back to hot sharking spots time and again. A Loran-C with a Plotter is one of the handiest instruments ever made. With a Plotter, one can troll back along a course where surface-finning sharks may have been seen earlier. A GPS works much like Loran-C, except that the GPS signal is beamed by satellite rather than from United States coastal towers, which gives it worldwide utility. As accurate as loran, GPS can pinpoint a spot on the ocean as small as 2 square meters. Any person venturing out to distant shark grounds beyond sight of land should have a good, working positioning device.

A reliable **depthsounder** should be part of the electronics arsenal. With the newer **LCD** (Liquid Crystal Display) sounders, a sharker can find productive bottom, structure, or active schools of baitfish anywhere along the water column. Many LCD depth machines also have a built-in **surface-water-temperature gauge**, indicating an area's shark potential. Separate water-temperature units are also available at a nominal cost.

A boat should have a 12-volt **VHF radio** for communications and emergencies. We also carry an additional **hand-held VHF** just in case the engine batteries go down. This past summer, we were invited to go sharking with an acquaintance who owned a 28-foot Rampage. Two miles below the headlands, Captain X realized he'd forgotten his charts. Five miles out, the loran went on the fritz. Upon reaching the shark grounds, our friend kept his radio and depth recorder on while we drifted with the engines off. When it was time to head

home, the engines wouldn't start. Luckily, we had a hand-held VHF to call the Coast Guard. We arrived back at the dock, in tow, at 11:30 that night, with a red-faced skipper and a very bored and hungry crew.

A **cellular telephone** is handy on the water, provided its batteries are up to snuff. If we want to privately report a secret hot spot to another angler, the cellular phone doesn't alert the whole fleet. It's also a great backup communications device. Many beginning fishermen wonder if all this fuss about costly electronics is just so much hype. But with the need to pinpoint position, depth, and water temperature, and to provide a safety line for emergency communications, today's anglers can't afford *not* to accumulate these gray and black boxes.

Sharking Gear

Through the years, anglers have found that a few well-chosen boat accessories can make

sharking easier. Foremost is a reliable **working anchor** for fishing in seas too uncomfortable for drifting. On the high-wind days when anglers simply cannot lay side-to in the trough, a good grapnel-type anchor on rocky bottom or a Danforth-type for mud or sand will save the trip.

The length of an anchor line, or *rode*, should be at least three times the depth of the water: 20 fathoms of water, 60 fathoms of line. A 10- to 12-foot length of ⅜- to ½-inch chain is usually shackled and trip-lined (see

A working anchor can be dropped and picked up later. If moving to another mark, use the boat's momentum and running poly-ball to break the anchor free from bottom. When the anchor is free, increase the rpm, and the ball will travel the length of the line, sliding up the anchor chain and holding the weight of the anchor while it's hauled back on board.

40" Poly-ball

Buoy

Bail

100-Fathom Line

accompanying illustration) between the anchor and the rode to help the anchor dig in.

Most sharking skippers use a 100-fathom coil of 9- or 12-thread pot warp (lobster- or crab-trap line) as a working rode, and keep it coiled in a large plastic laundry basket secured in the boat's bow area. A large (40-inch) **poly-ball** is used in-line, so that the anchor can be quickly released if the skipper must chase a large

hooked fish; a Styrofoam buoy tops off the anchor line's tag end. Try to purchase pot warp and poly-balls from a commercial fisheries supplier; they sell at lower prices than marine stores catering to yachtsmen.

Some skippers carry a **parachute sea anchor** for heavy-seas fishing and safety. A parachute sea anchor cleated forward will make angling much more comfortable when the sharking is good and the wind picks up. It's also deployed in the event of engine failure to prevent a boat from wallowing in the trough. A parachute sea anchor must be large enough to do the job: anything less than 4 feet in diameter will be ineffective.

Never use a sea anchor from a stern cleat. Heavy seas can wash over the transom, filling the boat with water. This illustration shows a parachute sea anchor placed incorrectly.

Many sportfishing boats come equipped with **outriggers**—very handy in shark fishing; a bait can be clipped to either rigger for slow-trolling. While chumming, we often use one rigger to keep our farthest bait from tangling with our mid-depth offering. Outriggers are not truly necessary for shark fishing; they just make it easier at times.

The same holds true for **downriggers**. A downrigger can drag a bait in the depths while you're slow-trolling—also inessential but handy. Both devices give anglers a wider latitude of fishing styles; and riggers, of course, are useful for other species too.

Safety on the Shark Grounds

Shark fishing is unique in its inherent danger. A bluefish can sever a finger, a billfish can swipe an arm; but a shark is the only gamefish that can eat you. Fortunately, that's a very rare and isolated occurrence.

In 1992, one of the Gulf of Maine's top shark-tuna skippers inadvertently found himself in the water at boatside with a 200-pound blue. The crew claimed the captain scrambled back aboard so fast that he was still dry from the waist up. Blue sharks and makos are notorious for biting a boat's chine or trim tabs when alongside, so they could be quite aggressive to a person.

Under normal conditions, shark angling is much safer than wading in a slippery trout stream. Just remember that your boatside quarry can instantly remove massive amounts of tissue. Handle sharks with the utmost respect.

When heading off to the shark grounds, make sure the radio works, the anchor is onboard, the **flares** and **life vests** are within easy reach, the hand-held VHF has fresh batteries, and all the safety equipment is in good order. Chances are you'll never need it, but adequate preparations can make the difference between arriving home late or not at all.

On the Beach

Some shark anglers want no part of this boat stuff. Australian Alfred Dean didn't need the perfect cockpit, outriggers, and chair to catch two of the largest sharks ever landed. These stupendous great whites, weighing in at 2,664 and 2,344 pounds, were taken from shore in the 1950s. Members of the Durban Angler's Club also fished from the sea wall near the old whaling station. Until the station closed, immense great whites were caught there on old-fashioned wooden reels and long, simple rods—like giant fly tackle.

Many sharks are taken by shore anglers along the Gulf Coast, where there are miles of unoccupied beach on the barrier islands. Sea walls and jetties make as good a platform for sharkers today as they did years ago. In 1964, while fishing from the Cherry Grove pier in South Carolina, Walter Maxwell caught an amazing 1,780-pound tiger. Maxwell's shark remains as the all-tackle world record for the species.

Farther south, Herb Goodwin pioneered beach angling for sharks along the east coast of Florida. According to Frank Woolner, Herb plucked some mighty hammerheads from the suds, and Goodwin was not a young man at the time. On-shore sharking will still nail a prize. In 1993, Mark Thawley caught a 350-pound sand tiger from South Carolina's Charleston Jetty, establishing a new all-tackle record for that species.

Abe Cuanang

Party boats often anchor over shark territory and are popular platforms for non-boatowners and visiting anglers. Here a big sevengill shark comes to wire on the Fury *in San Francisco Bay.*

Party Boats

Party boats are another way for non-boat-owners to get to sharky areas. A low-budget, full-day trip may climax with a nice shark swimming around the boat, and many skippers will allow a customer to bait it. Whether fishing from the *Yellow Bird* in the Gulf of Maine, the *Karen* in northern Scotland, or the *Venture* from San Diego, an angler may get a crack at Jaws, as a constant stream of bottom fish come over the rail—a prime method of tolling in big, active sharks.

3

TACKLE

Captain A.W. Lewis stands next to his historic sand tiger, caught on a pre-star-drag reel and split bamboo rod. The guide, Jose "Mexican Joe" Presiado, was one of California's first professional boatmen.

AND
TECHNIQUES

Modern sharking tackle has come a long way since the early days of the sport. The first rod-and-reel sharks were taken by turn-of-the-century anglers at Catalina Island, off the coast of California. Their reels had simple drag overrun systems, no free-spool or antireverse; and the rods were built from hickory and lancewood or from split bamboo. One of the first known shark anglers, Captain A. W. Lewis, used a simple 4/0 reel and wooden rod to catch a large ground shark at Santa Catalina around 1905. After the introduction of Bill Boschen's star drag in 1913, anglers finally had a tool capable of landing large fish without skinning their knuckles.

The star drag opened up a whole new world of angling: now a fish could rip line from the reel without the handle spinning backward. The most famous big-game angler of his time, Zane Grey, started fishing at Avalon, then explored the Mexican mainland, and moved out into the Indo-Pacific. In Australia, he caught six ground sharks in one day. His star-drag Coxe reel was up to the task, but Grey's wooden rod snapped in three places.

Wooden rods, with their penchant for breaking at the crucial moment, were used until after World War II. Then the first fiberglass rods hit the market, and the modern big-game rod was born. The best of these early E-glass rods were built by Californian John Harrington.

The earliest sharkers fought their fish standing up, wearing a simple leather fighting belt, in the stern of a 20-foot motor launch. Zane Grey sat in a gimbaled chair and used an old-fashioned shoulder harness. Today, we have returned to standing while fighting fish. The chair is reserved for those who battle the biggies.

Today's shark outfits and techniques have evolved over a span of more than 90 years. Glass rods now compete with graphite versions, and Boschen's star wheel has been superseded by the lever drag. Let's take a look at our choices in tackle and tactics.

Shark Rods

For medium-size fish, **boat rods** from 6½ to 7 feet long are good, inexpensive shark-fishing tools. Most boat models have standard stainless or ceramic "boat rod guides" and a matching tip-top. The number of guides on a rod usually reflects the quality of the piece, and a general rule of thumb is one guide for each foot of rod length. Rods with fewer guides should be relegated to codfish and calico bass.

Decent boat rods are equipped with a set of Fuji aluminum-oxide, ceramic guides and a strong graphite reel seat. Higher-quality boat rods often come with a gimbaled butt, for use with a fighting belt; these rods are often rated by line strength, such as "25–40 lb Test Line," usually printed somewhere on the lower part of the shaft. They may also carry an action rating, like "Medium-Heavy Action." For medium-size game, a boat model with the above ratings will turn the trick. If there's a chance of meeting up with the big brutes, consider moving up to a 50- to 80-pound (lb) rod.

Recently, we saw a "super boat rod" equipped with a roller "stripper" (lower) guide and a roller tip-top. The rest of the guides are standard ceramic guides. With roller guides at the two worst pressure points, your line will last longer, especially when you're fighting large fish. The small extra investment in a "super boat rod" is offset by savings in line. Because it is very forgiving, one of these rods in the 7-foot length is the best tool for beginning shark anglers.

Trolling rods with all roller guides and a roller tip-top are the most expensive saltwater models. These are "class" rods, rated to International Game Fish Association standards. A "30-lb Class" trolling rod is designed to flex best with line that breaks with 30 pounds of pull. This style of measurement is used by those who fish for world records.

When records are not the ultimate goal, an experienced angler may overline a trolling rod: use a stick rated for 30-lb with 40-lb test because the heavier line offers greater abrasion resistance, requiring fewer line changes. Line as heavy as 50-lb test, however, may exert too much strain on the blank, and the rod could break. Going up 10 pounds provides greater abrasion resistance, resulting in fewer line changes.

A 30-lb-class trolling rod is ideal for medium game; for makos, hammerheads, and threshers, a 50-lb-class rod will be handy; for the giant predators, one needs a rugged 80-lb- or even 130-lb-class rod. And when you hook old Megajaws, usually when you're after a much smaller animal, you'll appreciate the roller guides that are standard on all trolling sticks.

Prudent anglers check the guides periodically to make sure they're rolling. Seasonally, remove the roller assemblies and grease them. Reinstall the rollers, then pass line through the guides to ensure that every guide is in working order. Remember, cheap roller guides don't even roll, so when purchasing a trolling rod, look for Aftco guides.

Heavy trolling rods in the 80- to 130-lb class are available with an optional bent-butt section. Fished from a chair, the bent butt gives an angler about 30 percent more lifting power than the traditional straight butt. Whether straight or bent, trolling rods, with their longer butts, do not work well for stand-up angling.

The newest shark sticks are the **short-stroke stand-up rods**. This style originated with the long-range fishing boats in San Diego, which needed a powerful rod to give more leverage to headboat anglers without access to a chair. These West Coast–style rods are built in one piece, with Hypalon grips above and below the reel

Caught from Captain Barry Gibson's Shark IV, *this 265-pound mako was taken on a sporting 30-lb-test outfit. The 7-foot boat rod and lever-drag reel are ideal for beginning anglers.*

seat; the guide layout is similar to that on the "super boat rod."

Designed to give the angler maximum power, these short, 5½- to 6-foot stand-up rods have most of the bend in the upper third of the blank. With the left hand placed well up the foregrip of this powerful stick, an angler can exert 50 percent more force than with a conventional, parabolic 7-foot trolling model. East Coast anglers adapted the stand-up rod to their needs, adding a short, detachable Aftco aluminum butt and fully rollered guides.

Anglers using a stand-up rod can whip inordinately large fish. The one disadvantage of a short rod is difficulty setting the hook with a lot of line out. So when you use a stand-up rod, fish closer to the boat.

Rod Materials and Lengths

Shark-rod blanks may be made from fiberglass, graphite, or a composite of both. The lighter **graphite** sticks transmit the feel of a hooked fish right up to the angler's hand, but they cannot withstand sudden impact, such as slamming onto the cockpit rail, or collapse from wall failure. The **composite** blanks are hardier and can withstand rugged duty. The best heavy shark rods are built from **E-glass**

Rob Richardson fights his 414-pound, world-record porbeagle on a 50-lb-class stand-up rod, with the headlands of Pentland Firth in the background. The short, 5½-foot rod gives an angler a great advantage in leverage.

blanks. Most rod companies—including Fenwick, Penn, Sabre, and Cal Star—make a variety of boat and trolling rods in epoxy E-glass, which is very durable.

Many boat rods and most trolling models are built in a standard, 7-foot IGFA length. The extra length helps beginning shark anglers avoid line slack, and many seasoned sharkers also prefer the 84-inchers since they make it easier to set the hook on a fish when a lot of line is out in the chum slick. We use these rods with our charter customers, many of whom have never caught a shark before. After a little practice with the longer rod, anglers can switch to the short 5½-footers for advanced work.

Using short stand-up rods and the new harnesses (see "Standing Up to Sharks," page 38, for more on harnesses), anglers can move up to 50- and even 80-lb-test line and take big fish without the expense of a chair. The long and short of rod choice is that it's a matter of an angler's wallet and experience.

Shark Reels: A Big Choice

Any good shark rod deserves a good reel, and there's a big choice on tackle-store shelves. Our old standbys, the **star-drag models,** are better than ever. Today, Penn's space-age version of Boschen's drag can be seen in their Senator series, originally developed in 1932 by Otto Henzie. Shark anglers will find the 4/0 Wide Senator II, coupled with 30- to 40-lb-test line, to be a very good light-tackle reel.

The Penn 114HL 6/0 holds up to 500 yards of small-diameter 50-lb line and is an excellent medium-heavy shark reel. For heavier work and larger fish, the standard Senator 9/0 will accommodate an additional 200 yards of the same line. Some anglers spool the 9/0 with 80-lb-test line, just about the upper limit for stand-up angling. Even bigger brutes can be tamed with the 12/0, which holds 800 yards of 80-lb-test line, or the 14/0 model, spooling 800 yards of 130-lb Dacron. These large reels require a fighting chair and a bucket harness.

Star-drag systems are readily adjustable over a wide range. The Penn 113HLW, for example, can be used with several line strengths—30-, 40-, or even 50-lb-test line. With a star drag, we can jump an entire line class, not only from 30- to 50-lb-test, but from 50- to 80-lb line in the larger models.

The star drag's only drawbacks are its tendency to overheat when pushed to the limit and its difficulty in maintaining consistent drag pressure.

That being said, any angler who thinks a star-drag reel can't tame monster sharks should remember Zane Grey's 1936 Australian catches. Fishing out of Sydney, Grey took an 840-pound great white and a half-ton tiger shark using a reel equipped with an early star drag.

Lever-Drag Reels

To help provide consistent line pressure, the lever drag made its appearance in the 1930s. The original reels, as built by Fin-Nor, were too expensive for most anglers. The first affordable lever drag was finally introduced by Penn in their International series.

All lever drags are made with a wide *disk* and a stationary *plate*, located within the recess of the rear side-plate. As the lever is pushed forward, resistance progressively increases. The lever drag is more heat-resistant than the star drag, which makes for a smoother exit of line when a shark makes a long or fast run.

Affordable lever-drag reels available today range from light, graphite-framed models to extra-rugged, machined aluminum versions. Many lever-drag reels are built with dual gear ratios. The lower gear—with a speed ratio of less than 2 to 1 in most cases—can be a godsend when a large, stubborn shark sounds.

With its 475-yard capacity of 30-lb line, the Penn 45GLS is the least expensive lever drag on the market. It's a good light-tackle performer, with a one-piece graphite frame. Moving up in price, the Penn International series offers rugged aluminum con-struction. For light- and medium-tackle work, the 30TW (wide) and the larger 50TW hold an amazing amount of line: 600 yards of 30-lb and 850 yards of 50-lb line, respectively. Both reels are also available in two-speed models—the 30SW and the 50SW. For monsters, you have the International 80STW (holding 900 yards of 80-lb line) and the mucho expensivo 130ST, which takes 1,000 yards and dollars.

Toyo Shimano offers top-quality lever-drag reels at competitive prices and makes the largest selection of graphite-frame models, all with drag systems as smooth as Penn's. The Shimano TLD20 and TLD25 will handle lines in the 20- to

Ultimate stand-up shark outfits include a 30-lb rod, a graphite Beastmaster reel, and a beefy 80-lb rig with a machined-aluminum Tiagra 50W-LRS. Both reels offer dual gear ratios.

40-lb range. Stepping up to the two-speed models, the Shimano Beastmasters offer the same line capacities as the TLDs, plus the ease of a simple push-button gear change.

The new Tiagra by Shimano is equal to Penn's International series, and serious sharkers will appreciate the heat-resistant drag and the dual speed. For heavier shark work, the Tiagra 50 and 50W will hold 600 and 850 yards of line, respectively; and the Tiagra 80W will spool close to 1,000 yards of fine-diameter 80-lb Dacron.

Setting the Drag

Lever-drag reels have three settings: *free-spool*, *strike*, and *full*. The strike setting is usually 25 to 30 percent of the line's breaking point—between 12 and 15 pounds of pull for 50-lb-test line, for example. This setting is adjusted with a **drag scale** and the reel's "pre-set" dial. Good drag scales are made by Chatillon and Manley. The Manleys have a sliding Delrin ring that indicates the exact poundage of the pull.

To set the drag, move the lever to the strike position, with the rod at 45 degrees to approximate the average rod angle when a fish takes line. To warm up the drag plates, pull line from the reel as if trying to start a balky old outboard motor. Then using scales, pull line from the reel at fish speed, checking the amount of drag on the scale's ring. If it's too much or too little, return the lever to *free-spool*, adjust the preset knob, push the lever up to *strike*, and pull line from the reel again. When the drag seems to be at the correct setting, pull with the scale for several more runs just to make sure it's consistent.

Never set the drag until the reel has been exposed to the heat of the day. A cold reel, stored in the cuddy or salon, needs to have its drag plates warmed to the static temperature of normal sunlight in the cockpit. The strike setting will increase during a long battle and should be rechecked after any active sharks are taken or even after short periods of storage.

Even though lever-drag reels have a full-drag setting, new anglers should be cautious about moving the lever much beyond *strike*. If more drag is required, apply additional pressure with the fingers of your left hand. "Full" drag means just what it says; and after a fish makes a long run, the drag can pop the line. Experienced anglers, using long "headers" in front of their regular line (see Chapter 4), can creep toward full drag, but you can lose fish by moving the lever beyond *strike* while working with normal line.

Drag increases as the amount of line on a reel's spool decreases. If a shark takes a long run, slide the lever back toward *free-spool* just a tad to minimize line breakage. Sometimes a fish will make a ripping run from boatside, and the rod angle can be lowered to lessen drag. Get to know what a lever drag will do once it's adjusted to the strike setting. A lever-drag reel is a wonderful tool, but it is not infallible.

All lever-drag reels are designed for line-class angling. A Penn 30SW reel, fitted to a 30-lb-class rod, is calibrated to handle 30-lb-test line. The reel will operate within the limited range of perhaps 6 to 10 pounds of pull at the strike position. A significant increase in the strike drag setting to accommodate 50-lb-test line, will result in the loss of free-spool. Unlike the star-drag model, a lever-drag setting cannot compensate for the next larger line class.

Star drags are difficult to set to a predetermined poundage; and if the drag wheel is tightened or loosened, the setting is

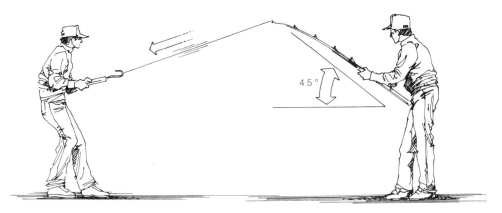

*Proper adjustment of a lever drag's strike setting is all-important. Work as a team,
pulling at least six runs while checking the scales and calibrating the pre-set.*

lost. Many anglers have developed a feel for the right amount of drag, especially those who fish just one line class.

Standing Up to Sharks

The superb drag system of the lever-drag reel is ideal for stand-up angling. Contemporary anglers have been "standing up to sharks" for a couple of decades, but the technique is not new. The father of stand-up fishing was William C. Boschen, who, from 1900 until his death in 1918, caught a variety of monster fish without using a chair or harness. With a 9/0 B-Ocean star-drag reel matched to a 24-thread rod, Bill Boschen used only a leather rod cup.

Today, we have a wide array of stand-up equipment available to us. New **fighting belts** and **harnesses** allow us to chase bigger sharks with each season, and shorter rods give us the extra leverage needed to handle these large brutes. The added mobility of the stand-up style gives anglers total freedom in playing a shark, and it's far more

exciting than sitting in a fighting chair.

An ideal **traditional light-tackle stand-up outfit** employs a 4/0W reel and a standard 7-foot boat or trolling rod with 30- to 40-lb-test line. Most stand-up sharkers replace their trolling rod's long Aftco butt with a shorter (12 inches) section, making the rod a little over 6½ feet long and moving the reel back to a comfortable position.

A **short-stroke light-tackle outfit** uses the same size reel with a 5-foot, 9-inch, stand-up rod, usually rated by the maker for 30- to 50-lb line. Both the traditional and short-stroke outfits are best matched to a sturdy, light fighting belt, such as the CYC Model TGB-1. If you need a harness, consider the CYC Model SUH-3—perhaps the finest of the light kidney harnesses available.

If there is a remote chance that large sharks may show up boatside, a **medium-heavy stand-up rig** can save the day. A 6/0 reel mounted on a 50- to 80-lb-test rod, usually 5½ feet long, is spooled with 50- to 60-lb-test line. If you're restricted to just one rod and reel, this is the combo to use. This outfit can increase pressure on both the angler and the fish, so heavier belts and harnesses are in order. Our favorite fighting belt is an aluminum model by Reliable, but the CYC Pro 2A Gimbal Belt is also a good choice. Both models offer a very secure gimbaled cup. Other good harnesses include The CYC Heavy Tackle Stand-Up Harness (SUH-2) and Braid's Power Play Harness.

At the upper limits of the sport, anglers fight monster sharks with a **heavy-duty stand-up combination**. Most of these rods are designed for 50- to 130-lb line and are fished with 80-lb test. Matching reels include the Penn 9/0 Senator, the Daiwa 900H, and the Tiagra 50WLRS. "LRS" stands for **Long Range Special**, and this Shimano 50-lb-class reel has a special 80-pound lever-drag system. An angler can exert tremendous force with these ultimate workhorse combos, and Harken has introduced a new body harness to help prevent back strain.

Whatever you buy, buy the best you can afford. Cheap, inferior rods and reels may fail—one of the most common causes of lost fish. Keep tackle failure to a mini-

mum by changing line often, oiling the reel and roller guides, and cleaning tackle with a light freshwater hosing after every outing.

Light-Tackle Basics

On the shark grounds, the designated angler should be wearing a **fighting belt** appropriate for 30-lb tackle. A **harness** pre-adjusted to the angler should be either worn or kept handy in case the quarry is too large to handle with a belt alone. After the shark has taken the bait and made a short run, pick the rod from the holder and slip the reel into gear. Keep the rod tip high; and as you feel the weight of the fish, let it pull the rod tip down to horizontal. When the weight of the fish has straightened the line, lift the rod briskly and vertically until there's a good bend in it.

Still keeping the weight of the fish on the rod, quickly "reel" the rod down to near horizontal, maintaining the bend. Repeat the hooking process by again sharply lifting

Using the pelvic tilt, the angler raises the rod by shifting the hips forward (left). *Line is gained by reeling the rod down as the hips shift aft* (right).

the rod close to vertical. This double hook set removes slack and stretch.

We suggest that anglers really hit a shark hard when setting the hook. Light mono stretches, making it difficult to bury the barb. Several years ago, during the first trip of the season, we had an angler pick up a rod and twitch it at a taking fish. Seconds later, a mako cleared the water in a classic jump and tossed the hook. The angler's hook-setting experience had all been on trout.

Your shark should now be well hooked and making its initial run, peeling line from the reel at a good clip. At this point drop the rod butt into the belt's gimbal cup, and keep the rod tip up, between 30 and 60 degrees, with plenty of pressure on the rod hand. Grasp the rod's foregrip at the most comfortable position near the top of the grip. When the shark stops running, start pumping the fish back to the boat. Stand-up practitioners lift the rod by pivoting or tilting their pelvis forward. This raises the rod tip at least 30 degrees, and you can quickly reel the rod down again, always ensuring that you feel the full weight of the hooked fish. As you take a few turns on the reel handle, let your pelvis shift backward as you lower the rod tip toward the fish. This style of pumping, the most efficient method of fighting fish regardless of species or size, owes its current popularity to our teacher Marsha Bierman, an expert billfisher and an international proponent of release-fishing. With light tackle, the angler's left hand becomes the fulcrum of the "pump." As the left arm pumps the rod in conjunction with the pelvic tilt, pressure on the fighting belt may decrease, and the rod could slip out of the gimbal pin or snap out of the cup. To avoid this, keep some downward pressure on the rod. To remove strain on your upper

The longer 30-lb boat rod, fitted with a gimbal and coupled to a 4/0W star-drag reel, makes a good rig for youngsters. Using such an outfit, this beginning angler took her first shark, a 75-pound blue whaler.

back, keep your body vertical. To lessen biceps fatigue, straighten your left arm whenever a shark runs and even during pumping.

This is the method we use with our sharking clients: throughout the pumping process, concentrate on "reeling" the rod down so that you maintain a good bend in the rod tip and avoid line slack. An angler should use a harness if tethered to a fish weighing more than 100 pounds. With a harness clipped onto the reel lugs, the reel becomes the fulcrum of the pelvic "pump."

This removes all strain from the angler's upper back and shifts the weight to the lumbar region.

With the harness holding the rod's weight, the left hand is freed for other duties. As the shark makes another run, you can lean back a bit and almost relax. When the fish stops running and it's time to pump it back, use the left hand to guide the line back onto the reel spool. Always try to keep the line level on the spool, so that a crown doesn't build up and jam against the reel's pillars or frame. Press the palm and fingers of your left hand against the spool to apply an additional 5 pounds of drag on a running fish. Be careful of line burn, however. The left hand on the reel can also help control the outfit if the line suddenly breaks, which can sometimes cause the rod to jump up toward the angler's face.

A stand-up angler equipped with a harness can exert a tremendous amount of pressure on a fish. With a proper-fitting belt and harness, more than 30 pounds of pressure can be exerted with 50- or 80-lb-test tackle. Amazingly, the system allows many anglers with chronic bad backs and knees (like me) to take fish they may be unable to fight in a chair.

During the fight, an angler can follow the movements of the shark by walking around in the cockpit. In smaller craft, the bow area often becomes a stand-up angler's arena. As the fish gets closer to the boat, the angler can shorten the pumping stroke to match a single turn of the reel handle. This series of quick, short-stroke pumps maintains momentum, hauling the shark ever closer to the boat and keeping the fish from getting its head.

Sooner or later, the fish will tire and

An 8-foot West Coast boat rod is ideal for midweight requiems, such as this soupfin shark taken by Abe Cuanang just west of Alcatraz Island.

Angelo Cuanang

can be pumped close alongside for release.

This basic light-tackle stand-up technique works for other fish, such as billfish and tuna. Whatever the fish, the two most important points are to let the harness do the dirty work and to maintain relentless pressure on the fish—never let it rest. With heavier tackle, belts, and harnesses, stand-up anglers can tame truly huge sharks. Practice is the key: as you gain experience in the harness, the fish become easier to handle.

RIGGING

This mako sports teeth that can bite through mono and smaller wire— a good reason for substantial wire leaders.

FOR SHARKS

Due to their sharp teeth, sharks require specialized rigging; and like most other species of big game, they often require additional reel drag during the finale. An angler's choice of lines and leaders, and even the way they are rigged, can make the difference between lost fish and success. So let's look at a few line, hook, and leader systems that give you the advantage on the shark grounds.

Line for Light and Medium Tackle

For light and medium tackle, monofilament line is a good choice. Pick a brand of **premium mono** that has consistent strength (no weak spots), good knot strength, and abrasion resistance. Many lines—such as Ande "Pink," Berkley "Big Game," Jinkai, Momoi, Fenwick's "Saltline," and Shakespeare's "Ugly Big Water Line"—have the qualities needed for sharking. All of these monofilaments will usually break above their pound-test rating. As your experience builds, you may

try for a world record. If you do, use IGFA "class" line, which breaks *at* its rated test, not above it. Class, or "tournament," line is manufactured by Ande, Amilan, Maxima, and Berkley.

The Double Line

To increase line strength at the fighting end, savvy anglers double the line for the first 15 to 20 feet ahead of the leader. Some anglers like the **Spider hitch** for this, but it can't take sudden impact. A much better knot, the **Bimini twist**, has a strength of almost 100 percent of the line's rating and is the only doubling knot we recommend.

After you have doubled the line, attach a snap-swivel using an offshore swivel knot or a Uniknot. Clip on a leader, and you're ready to go sharking. With several wraps of the double line back on the reel, you have effectively doubled the strength of the mono. If you're using 50-lb test, for instance, the line now has a strength of 100 pounds in the forward section where it's most needed.

The Bimini twist.

(A) Double the line
to the desired length and
have a helper hold it about 3
feet away. Pass the 3-foot tag
end and standing line around
each other 20 times, and
tighten the 20 twists
toward each other.

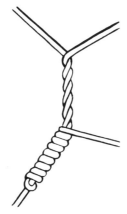

(B) Each person exerts
equal tension until the twists
"harden" at about 2 inches
long; then relieve the tension
on the tag end, keeping it
at just over 90 degrees to the
twists. It will roll back over
the twists neatly (when you've
had some practice).

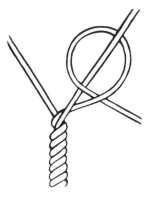

(C) Once the tag rolls to
the doubled line, hold the
knot with finger and thumb,
and take a half-hitch
around one line.

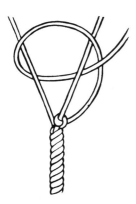

(D) Make a second half-hitch
over both lines.

(E) Finish the knot by making
a loop with three turns passing under it (triple half-hitch).

(F) Carefully pull the loop
tight, and trim to within
¼ inch of the finished knot.

Courtesy IGFA

The offshore swivel knot.

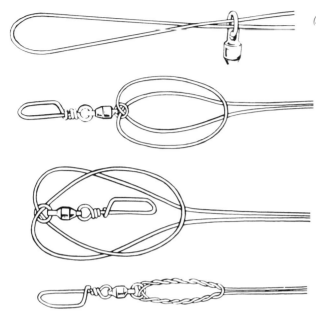

Courtesy IGFA

(A) Slide the snap-swivel up the doubled line, making one twist in the loop.

(B) Bring the loop back over the swivel and doubled line.

(C) Pass the swivel through the loop and double the line six times.

(D) Moisten the twists with saliva; pull tight, using thumb and forefinger or pliers.

The Uniknot.

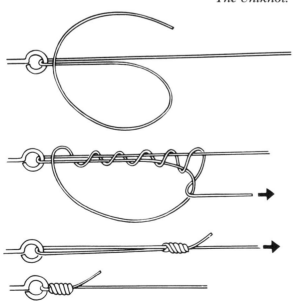

Courtesy IGFA

(A) Pass 12 inches of single or doubled line through the snap-swivel, making a circle, with the tag end pointing back up toward the rod tip.

(B) Using your middle fingers to keep the line apart, make six wraps with the tag end through the circle and around the double line.

(C & D) Pull the tag end to tighten, but not too much. Then pull the double line to slide the knot down to the swivel eye, seating the knot with thumbnail pressure.

The loop splice.

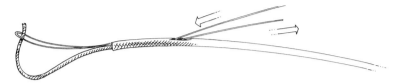

(A) Double a length of light leader wire, crimping it to make a "splicing needle."
Double the Dacron line to the desired length, insert the needle into the line toward
the loop end, push it inside for 3 inches, then bring it back out.
Catch the Dacron end with the needle, pulling it back through the line.

(B) Detach the line end from the needle and repeat another 3-inch section, exiting
½ inch above the first splice, catching the line end and bringing it back through. Repeat.
Trim the end close and fuzz it with your fingers, tightening the splice in both directions.

(C) Seize with dental floss at each exposure, using a series of six half-hitches,
six wraps, six half-hitches, and so on, finishing with a triple half-hitch.

The loop-to-loop connection.

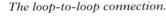

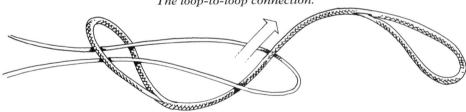

Slip the header loop over the end of the doubled line, and pull the other end
of header through until tight. For snap-swivels, slip the header loop through
the swivel-eye, and pull the swivel through.

Venezuela Rig

To further strengthen the business end of a line, you can add a 130-lb **Dacron header** to the front of the doubled line. The 15-foot-long header, with a loop splice at each end, is attached between the doubled line and the snap-swivel by a **loop-to-loop connection.** We now go from 50-lb test, to 20 feet of doubled line for 100-lb test, to 15 feet of 130-lb Dacron. This handy configuration was developed by Venezuelan skippers as a buffer against shark abrasion. It will slip through Aftco heavy-duty rod guides to the reel. For proper strength and insurance, wrap the Dacron splice with dental floss to keep it from slipping.

The Bimini twist and Dacron header work great with light to medium tackle and 30- to 50-lb-test monofilament lines. If you're after records, make sure the double-line/header combo doesn't exceed IGFA limits. Consider the header as part of the leader, and keep it short; the entire wire leader and header should be no longer than 30 feet.

Line for Heavy Tackle

We recommend **Dacron line** for heavy tackle, either the 80-lb stand-up system or 80- to 130-lb outfits used with a fighting chair. In these heavier sizes, mono's large diameter makes for an outsized Bimini twist.

Aftco "Big Foot" roller guides, standard equipment on most heavy trolling rods, will pass the Dacron line's Bimini knot with no problem. With 80-lb stand-up gear, smooth line passage calls for a Dacron loop splice. The long loop becomes the double line, and is made with three extralong tucks, also seized with dental floss.

The Mono Header

Another way to increase the strength of Dacron end-line is to splice in a 100-yard length of heavy monofilament leader material. This is the method we use and recommend. For 80-lb Dacron, a length of 125-lb-test mono can be inched into the hollow core until about 12 feet is buried

inside the braided line; then seize the first 5 inches of each end of the area with floss. This **header-splice** works like the Chinese Finger Trap that has fascinated children for centuries, and allows a smooth transition to a greater line strength. But before attempting the mono header, remove the sharp cut at the end of the leader material with a fine file or sandpaper.

With 130-lb Dacron, either 200- or 250-lb-test mono (depending on the manufacturer's thickness) can be slowly worked into the braid.

This abrasion-resistant method of doubling line strength for large sharks is very handy indeed for general fishing. It's not for record-seekers, though, because the splice is considered part of the leader. When attaching a snap-swivel, use two crimping sleeves with a snug fit and a matching crimping tool. An in-line **plastic bead** ahead of the crimps will eliminate damage to roller-tips, often caused by reeling crimps into the tip-top.

Snaps and Swivels

Something as simple as an incorrect snap-swivel can make the difference between landed and lost fish; every season a great number of sharks escape due to weak or defective swivels. Foremost in the non-working-swivel department is the common **Rosco**, formed with a single barrel and two eyes by a non-tempered swaging process that is weak by design. We recommend this style of swivel only for light-tackle applications, such as 20- to 30-lb-test gear and smaller sharks. Roscos should not be used for trolling because, under pressure, they just don't rotate.

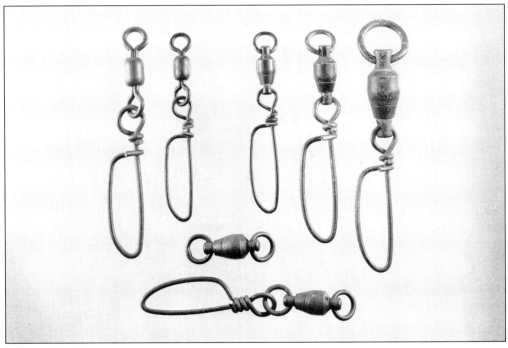

Rosco snap-swivels (left), sizes 7 and 6, are fine for light-tackle chumming. Sampo ball-bearing snap-swivels (right), sizes 6 to 8, will hold up to heavy fish and trolling. Below: a Sampo in-line swivel for leaders, and a top-notch double-ring snap-swivel.

All swivels are rated for a certain poundage, tested under ideal, in-house conditions. The actual strength of the snap could be far less; sharkers should use larger snap-swivels than might seem adequate.

Aboard the *Lucky Star II,* we choose snap-swivels by their ring size, always making sure that a swivel's ring cannot enter and fetch up in a rod's tip-top. A few years ago, one of our stand-up anglers tied into a 350-pound brute that came to wire before deciding to make one last run. The angler cranked the snap-swivel into the rod's roller-tip, it jammed tight, and he was almost hauled overboard before the swivel popped free—a lesson for us all.

Over the years, certain styles and sizes have withstood both the battle and the final wiring. Rugged Sampo ball-bearing swivels rotate easily, even under the pressure of trolling. With a brazed ring on one end and a formed-wire **Coastlock snap** on the other, these strong connectors will stand up to the largest of beasts. Murray Brothers of Riviera Beach and the Rite Angler in Fort Lauderdale sell an improved style of ball-bearing Sampo with a brazed ring at each end. This "better mouse trap" is less likely to kink around itself, an occasional problem with single-ringed Sampos.

Sampo also sells quality double-ringed ball-bearing swivels fitted with the **McMahon snap**, which looks like a miniature scissor shackle. The McMahon snap has been around a long time, and is favored by many experienced skippers and wire-men. The McMahon provides a positive method of securing a leader, it can be grabbed safely during wiring, and it avoids the Coastlock's tendency to "open up" during battle.

For light-tackle work in the 30- to 40-lb-test range, we like to use a #5 or #6 snap-swivel. For medium-heavy, 50- to 60-lb line, a #7 is a good choice. And for the "big guns" in the 80- to 130-lb category, a #8 snap-swivel is essential. Most snap-swivels and swivels are available in a flat black finish, usually sold under the prefix "BX." We like flat black for all saltwater work. Plain black swivels, sans snap, are very handy for rigging a two-part mono-to-wire leader system.

Single-Wire Leaders

Because of the nature of the beast, heavy monofilament leaders just don't cut it. For most sharks we prefer single-strand-wire leader material, and **strong stainless wire** is readily available. Years ago, sharkers made their leaders from tungsten piano wire, which is actually stronger than equal-diameter stainless, but it rusts within days into a useless coil of brown scale.

Good stainless material is sold by American Fishing Wire and by Malin, which still makes the traditional piano-wire stuff as well. Most stainless wire is tinted a coffee color to help camouflage your offerings. After just a bit of use, the Malin wire starts to turn shiny; but the American brand seems to keep its brown color for several outings. Either brand works well.

Depending on the quarry and the size of their tackle, shark fishermen will find an ideal working leader material in the #7 to #15 sizes. Number 9 wire breaks at 95 pounds of pull, #13 single-strand at 195 pounds, and #15 at 240 pounds. We reuse a leader until it becomes too short or develops a kink.

The Haywire Twist

Shark anglers unknowingly borrow from other occupations to rig their leaders. The farmers gave us the *haywire twist*, which isn't a Country-Western dance but a way of tying wire into a proper knot. We borrowed pliers originally used by cowpokes of the American West for fencing the open range. With wire from the music industry, we use the cowboy's tool to help form a farmer's twist. "Yippee ki yi yea, don't step in the melon patch but hand me the **fishing pliers**, Cappy!"

All single-strand leaders are constructed with the haywire twist. For those sharkers who have trouble wrapping a strong and neat twist, the Dubro Company offers an easy-to-use Haywire Twist Tool that will do the trick.

The great advantage of single-strand stainless wire is its small diameter and ease of use. An inadvertent kink in this material, however, will break the leader. Also, heavier sizes (#13 and up) are very stiff.

Double-Strand Leaders

To overcome the stiffness of large-diameter leaders, you can combine two lighter strands of stainless to form a heavier trace. It works well and is surprisingly flexible.

The haywire twist.

(A) *Run 6 inches of wire through the hook-eye and make a loose loop so the hook will swing freely. Wed the wire in 6 to 8 short, equal, X-shaped turns of the standing wire and the tag end.*

(B) *Roll the tag end in four, tight, barrel turns. Bend the tag into an L-shaped handle and rotate the wire to break it at the barrel turns. Do not snip the tag with pliers. Repeat steps to make a loop at the other end of the leader to attach it to the snap-swivel. Pliers help hold the loop while you're forming twists on this end (gaps in twists exaggerated for clarity).*

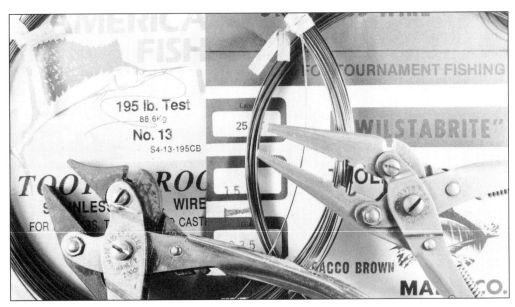

Quality wire and pliers are essential for sharking success and safety. Most good pliers with lasting "snipability" are made in Great Britain. When wiring sharks, wear your pliers at all times.

A double-strand wire leader.

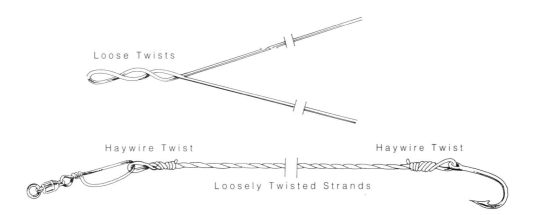

Loose Twists

Haywire Twist   Haywire Twist

Loosely Twisted Strands

Unroll about 35 feet of #10 to #12 wire, snip it from the leader coil, and run both tag ends back to find the center. Fold and pinch this point of the wire, making two legs 17½ feet long, and chuck the bent end into a cordless drill. While one person runs the drill at a slow speed, a second person keeps the two long ends from tangling while feeding the "twist" into the leader.

The finished product—which is easier to make than it sounds—is attached to the hook with a haywire twist. The other end is finished the same as a single-strand leader: make a loop for the snap-swivel by twisting in another haywire wrap. The double-strand leader is tougher to trim with the finish turn and resists making a clean break. As expected, the leader is less prone to kink and is much more flexible than a single-strand leader.

Multi-Strand Traces

Some sharkers who hunt extremely large sharks favor leaders made from 49-strand

fishing cable. Although it requires mechanical crimps and a proper crimping tool, it's less apt to kink than single-strand. When using cable, make sure that the crimps and the tool are the proper size for the leader wire, which can vary from 300- to 600-lb test. For a stinger rig, slide an additional crimp on the cable before you start rigging. The second hook, on a short length of multi-strand, can be adjusted farther up the leader to the length of any baitfish, crimped in place, and trimmed.

Many Australian shark anglers swear by massive plastic-coated clothesline cable for great whites. For small sharks and for casting, light-duty cable, usually found with a black plastic covering, is also handy.

Surf Leaders

Shore-based anglers after large sharks must overcome obstacles that boat folks don't worry about. To get the baits to drift out past the surf, where the sharks are, beach fishermen need an offshore wind, an ebbing tide, or a kite. Typically, large wind-resistant floats carry the bait beyond the breakers,

Crimping mono and wire.

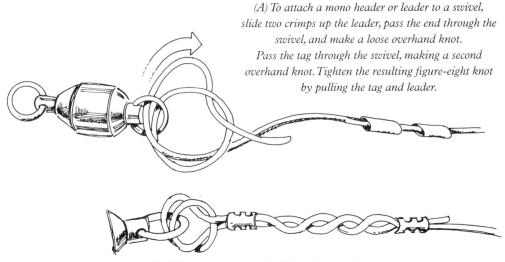

(A) To attach a mono header or leader to a swivel, slide two crimps up the leader, pass the end through the swivel, and make a loose overhand knot. Pass the tag through the swivel, making a second overhand knot. Tighten the resulting figure-eight knot by pulling the tag and leader.

(B) Slide a crimp close and tight, and crimp it. Twist the leader and tag until you've got 3 inches of twist and press on second crimp. For a 49-strand wire leader, use a figure-eight knot for the hook and the loop at the other end of the leader, with two crimps at each end. Thimbles are optional.

and leaders must be short or the bait will fetch bottom on the way out through the surf line.

To get around this, leaders are rigged in two parts, with each wire passing through one swivel eye of the other leader. With the leaders parallel, the upper swivels are lashed together with light line or dental floss. When a shark is hooked, this temporary lashing parts, and the leaders slide out to their full length.

The Mono/Wire Leader

Monofilament and wire can be combined to produce an excellent leader. Originally developed by shark specialists in the Carolinas and Great Britain, the two-part trace features a 10- to 12-foot length of heavy (300- to 400-lb test) mono leader attached to a rugged ball-bearing swivel (no snap). A 5- to 6-foot length of single- or multi-strand wire is wedded to the other end of the swivel, and a swinging hook is attached to the business end. The upper monofilament leader section is crimped much like 49-strand cable or the mono header.

After a couple of sharks have been taken and released, the short forward section is cut off and replaced with new wire. Even with some abrasion, the upper mono section can be used repeatedly. The mono/wire leader is not only a cost-cutting device but also a very pragmatic one since the free-rolling ball bearing keeps tangles to a minimum, especially when hooked up to active jumping sharks such as the mako. Anyone who has wired a fish with a

A standard mono/wire leader.

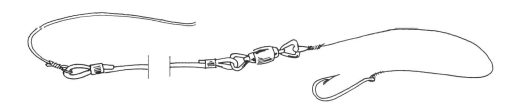

mono/wire leader knows that it is much easier on the hands than other styles. One of the few drawbacks of this system: a fish that swings around and bites the upper, mono portion of the leader will be lost.

Whatever type of leader you choose, make sure that all haywire and mono-crimp connections are positive, and check the leader after every fish for stress points or kinks. Long leaders, usually 15 to 18 feet, are important, especially when you're fishing for species that roll the leader and may be long enough to abrade line during the fight, or turn and bite the line if the leader is too short. Leaders and swivels are two of the primary connectors between the shark and the angler. The third connection—the hook—is perhaps the most important single item in your arsenal.

Popular Shark Hooks

Shark anglers around the world use a wide variety of hook styles. Hooks are made by O. M. Mustad in Norway, perhaps the oldest manufacturer of saltwater hooks in continuous operation; by VMC in France; by Eagle Claw in the United States; and by Gamakatsu in Japan. Because they're ubiquitous, we'll concentrate on Mustad hooks;

similar patterns are available from other companies.

The popular O'Shaughnessy pattern—named after its designer, an Irish hookmaker—has been borrowed and modified by many other manufacturers. This 1X-strong ring-eye hook is adequate for tackle up to the 30-lb class. Try to stop a big fish with 50-lb tackle, however, and the 1X O'Shaughnessy will open up. Choose a 2X-strong hook for heavier gear.

We use the light-wired O'Shaughnessy for release angling because the shank will rust and leave the fish faster than a heavy-wire hook, especially if the barb is pinched down with a pair of pliers. We recommend **tinned** or **cadmium-plated hooks** rather than stainless steel. A shark will carry a stainless hook forever. For many applications, particularly when you're fishing for smaller sharks, O'Shaughnessys in the 7/0 to 12/0 sizes work fine. All hooks, regardless of style or wire strength, should match the size of your bait without showing a high profile.

Mustad has a short-shanked, 2X-strong, O'Shaughnessy-bend hook—the No. 9174—which works well with light and medium tackle in the 30- to 50-lb-test range. It comes in a **bronzed finish** that's great for release angling since it rusts away faster than tinned versions. We use this

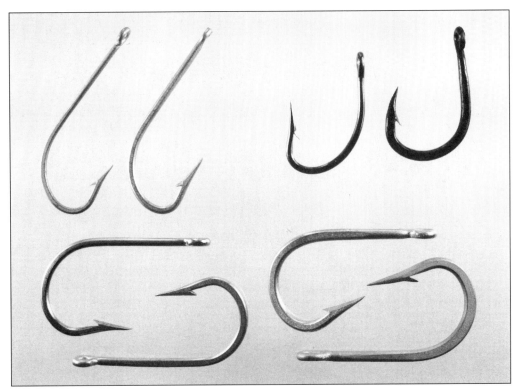

The O'Shaughnessy and 2X-stout needle-eye version (upper left) are good 20- to 40-lb-class shark hooks. Short-shanked live-bait hooks (upper right) include a bronzed Mustad and stronger Gamakatsu. Heavier shark hooks, like the Sea Demon and the offset-point (lower left), are 2X-strong. For big fish, 3X-strong hooks (lower right) include the reverse offset and the traditional Sobey.

camouflaged hook for live baiting sharks.

The forged Sobey or "Southern & Tuna," No. 7690, is one of our strongest hooks. And with its needle or brazed-ring eye, it costs an arm and a leg. Two Sobey-style hooks are very popular with shark aficionados: The 2X-Strong No. 7699 has a brazed ring-eye and a **Kirbyed offset point** (named for Charles Kirby, a 17th-century London hookmaker); Eagle Claw has a close version with a non-brazed eye—their No. 9015. A very similar hook, the Mustad No. 7698R, has a brazed eye and a **reverse**

Kirby offset. Its wire size is 3X-strong, making it THE HOOK for monster hunters. We use these two hooks, sizes 8/0 to 14/0, for all heavy shark angling.

"Browning" and Sharpening Hooks

Light-wire hooks set easier with light tackle than heavy-wire hooks, which require heavier tackle and greater pressure but, on the other hand, won't pull or tear out of the

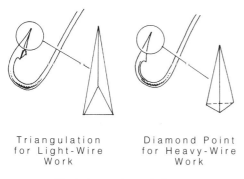

Triangulation
for Light-Wire
Work

Diamond Point
for Heavy-Wire
Work

Hook sharpening techniques.

shark's mouth so easily. Pick a few patterns that are ideal for your sharking needs and remove that just-out-of-the-box shine (which may repel wary fish) by "browning" them. Drop the hooks into a can of Clorox and salt water and leave them there for a few days to dull the plating.

Next, sharpen those babies to a razor point. A small, metal mill file works well and does the job quickly. Hit just the point; do not sharpen the length of the barb or the hook will ride, or cut a groove inside the

shark's mouth until it finally pulls out. There are two ways to sharpen a hook: *Triangulation* sharpens the point to the same angles cut by the hookmaker. The two upper surfaces and the lower surface of the point are filed until the hook is sharp enough to hang on a thumbnail. The *diamond point* hones the two upper surfaces and forms the lower two into a mirror image. Triangulate 1X-strong hooks and those with light wire for effective penetration, but sharpen larger hooks and heavy-wire hooks using the diamond point.

Both methods work well. The important thing is that you remember to sharpen your hooks, not only initially but after use. And when a file finally turns into a mass of crud, chuck it in the dumpster and buy a new one. Nothing is more frustrating than trying to sharpen a hookpoint with a nasty, dull file.

We have chosen a selection of terminal tackle that will work anywhere, for any size fish. Now let's jig or troll up some baitfish and set the table.

5 PREPARING

Pictured in 1926, boatman Francis Arlidge readies a lip-hooked kahawai for New Zealand makos. The baitfish is also plentiful in South Australian waters and feeds on krill.

AND SERVING THE MEAL

One of the most important and enjoyable aspects of any form of big-game angling is catching your own fresh bait. Recently, I had the opportunity to "make bait" aboard the *Patriot,* a luxury long-range party boat out of San Diego. In the middle of the night, under the Mexican skies at Guadeloupe Island, the mate and I turned on the halogen lights and attracted schools of Pacific scad within jigging distance. We caught scads all right, but we also dropped a few live baits to the bottom—just to see what night creatures were down there. Within an hour we managed to hook and land two curious horned sharks.

Think of shark baits just as you think of your own food. We salivate at the thought of fish fresh enough to become sushi or seviche. Fresh iced fish from a coastal market can tempt our palate, but it's not the same as just-caught. And then there's the frozen stuff, fish sticks—dry, flavorless, and chewy.

We have different reactions to these three forms of fare, and so do sharks. The old school of thought—a shark will eat anything—still has its apostles. But more and

more we discover that some sharks can be downright fussy. So we should do our best to present an appealing and tasty meal, remembering that sharks prefer oilier fish than we do.

A Gourmet Spread: Catching and Keeping Live Bait

Successful sharkers know that nothing entices a fussy fish like a lively, wiggling baitfish. Some species, like porbeagles, home in on live fare to the exclusion of everything else. Threshers, another active species, prefer a bait sending out distress signals. Big, smart makos often pick up live baits after passing by dead ones, as do mature blue sharks, in our experience.

Anglers need a way to keep their baits alive, from the time they're caught until the boat settles down on the shark grounds. Many sportfishing boats are factory-equipped with built-in baitwells.

Portable live-bait tanks are available commercially too, but a homemade version can be built for a fraction of the cost.

We catch our live baits at coastal hot spots before heading offshore. No matter where you live, kicking baits are available if you check out inshore haunts. Usually found in shallow regions and over shoals,

A Do-It-Yourself Portable Live-Bait Tank

Live-bait tanks are one of the handiest aids at the sharker's disposal, and they don't have to cost an arm and a leg. Aboard the *Lucky Star II*, we installed a serviceable baitwell by starting with an existing 12-volt, on-demand saltwater wash-down system, already hooked to a standard hose-thread marine faucet.

We also used a 32-gallon plastic trash can, ⅝-inch-O.D. and ¾-inch-O.D. plastic thru-hulls, a length of garden hose (⅝-inch I.D.), a length of ¾-inch-I.D. plastic hose, a tube of silicon sealant, and a couple of stainless hose clamps.

Starting with a ⅝-inch drill, we installed the smaller thru-hull about 4 inches up from the bottom of the trash can, caulking it well with silicon to prevent leaks. With a ¾-inch drill, we then installed the second thru-hull about 10 inches down from the top, again waterproofing with sealant. Next we connected the lower (intake) hose to the thru-hull with a hose clamp. We hand-tightened the other end, a standard-thread female hose-fitting, to the wash-down faucet. We clamped the upper (out-take) hose to the ¾-inch thru-hull, and trimmed it to allow the exiting water to empty overboard from the cockpit.

Captain Matt Wilder and I spent about $35 and a couple of off-hours putting this baitwell together. When filled with seawater from the wash-down-faucet valve, this inexpensive portable tank can keep a dozen large baits lively for a day of shark fishing. When not in use, it can be disconnected and stored at the dock.

baitfish readily hit jigs; multiple feathers; or Christmas trees, little quills spaced on a light monofilament rig; or tiny gold hooks ganged on even lighter mono. In the United Kingdom similar feathers will take baits inshore or on the shark grounds.

Members of the mackerel and scad families are found in every ocean. These active baitfish require plenty of oxygen to keep them kicking, but they are among the very best baits obtainable. The families include the **Atlantic** (or Boston) **mackerel**, the **Pacific mackerel**, the **bigeyed scad** (goggle-eye), the Bahamian **cero**, the **Pacific scad**, and the **sierra mackerel**. In a good bait tank, a high percentage of macks and scads will live through a day's angling. Remove the dead and dying, and ice them down as the next best thing.

In the American Northeast, **menhaden** (also called mossbunkers or pogies) and smaller **bluefish** (snappers) make excellent live baits. After locating a school of bunker, snag individuals with a weighted treble hook (available at most coastal tackle shops). Pogies are hardy, and will live in an aerated tank for several days. They are eagerly taken by porbeagles, blue sharks, and makos. A lively bluefish, around 4 to 8 pounds, is one of the very best mako baits. Other sharks will home in on this species, of course, but anglers after a trophy mackerel shark use bluefish when they're available.

Bonito and **little tunny**, found in both the Pacific and Atlantic, and also the **kahawai**, a weakfishlike species of Australia and New Zealand, make good larger baits. These pelagic schooling fish often enter shallow water, less than 100 feet deep. Like bluefish, they'll hit trolled artificials, such as a Jaw Breaker or a Rapala CD-13 or -18. Or you can cast to a surfaced school with shiny spoons, such as the Kastmaster. Kahawai,

Captain Barry Smith displays one of the best mako baits—a live bluefish. Alive or dead or even slabbed, a 3- to 6-pound blue in the chum slick is tough to beat.

often located under a mass of working terns, are readily taken on metal spoons.

Large offerings like bluefish, bonito, **skipjacks**, and tunny require special handling; many fishermen wrap these prized live baits in a wet towel or place them in the livewell, then run their boats at face-contorting speeds for the deeper shark waters. Off the coast of Florida, where little tunny and small blues are abundant during the winter months, the baitfish is hooked to a shark leader and fished in the same area it was caught. It doesn't take long for a bull shark to come sniffing around.

Live baits are often jigged up right on the shark grounds and transferred directly to the shark rigs. In the Metro area and the

Gulf of Maine, anglers can jerk for **codfish** while drifting for sharks. Live **herring** are often snagged by the same big diamond jigs, and a kicking silvery herring or tempting cod is definitely gourmet fare for blue, thresher, and mackerel sharks. U.K. sharkers "feather" **pilchards** and **coalfish**, which are relished by porbeagle and blue sharks.

If you happen to drift over a patch of mud bottom, you'll find a variety of benthic dwellers that are taken by sharks. **Whiting** and **hake** are found over soft mud, and both species make *decent* live baits. Tuna seem to crave both fish. But because they tend to bloat and die easily, becoming bobbers, they're not particularly attractive to sharks.

A chum slick often attracts little tack mackerel in the Northeast, and tinkers off California and the British Isles. A tack is small for a bait, but with a light-wired O'Shaughnessy, it can be presented to schoolie blue sharks, little mackerel sharks, and tope. We've also found **squid** in the slick, and taken them with a multipronged squid jig. If it's alive, we try it, no matter what its size or shape.

Years ago, when most fishermen, including me, thought that makos just didn't visit the Gulf of Maine, Captain Skip Stinson and I went out to the Monhegan ground for a day of blue sharking. Using light, 20-lb tackle, we set out two fresh baits and a live mackerel right at the boat and started chunking. It was a slow day until a very active shark nailed the live mackerel with an impressive turn of speed.

Skip fought the fish and I wired it, and we brought the "porbeagle" into Brown Brothers Wharf, where our local guru, Captain Arno Rogers, exclaimed in his deep, knowing voice, "You caught a mako, boys." We never would have hooked that fish if we'd been dunking only dead baits.

Home Cookin': Preparing Fresh Fish

Even today, there are many weathered skippers who believe that freshly dead baits are "good 'nough." We consider such fare an acceptable second choice. After all, there are those terrible days when you can't seem to catch a live bait to save your soul. When we tire of spending precious time trolling barren waters for macks that were plentiful the day before, we reach into the cooler and retrieve the iced mackerel that expired in the bait tank the day before. Any of the baitfish species we've mentioned can become appealing home cookin'.

Anglers without access to a live-bait tank must use fresh dead bait as their only offering. A few tricks in its initial preparation can make it more attractive. Place freshly caught or expired baitfish in a plastic bag before immediately laying them on ice in a cooler. This retains the bait's lifelike color. If the fish is tossed directly onto the ice, the fresh water will fade the natural hues. And if the fresh bait is simply tossed into a bucket without being iced, the heat of the day and the fish's internal digestive process will soften the flesh.

On the fishing grounds, fresh baits are sometimes available from draggers or gillnetters after they haul back. If the skipper is a friend, ask for a tray of his shack fish, or jog around the vessel and scoop up floaters with a landing net. Granted, this shack may not be in the very best condition, but it beats frozen bait. The largest blue shark we have caught and subsequently released was taken on a large, mirrorlike shad that came directly from a gillnetter's shack tray.

Remember, shark anglers use freshly

dead baitfish far more often than any other bait. The way they're preserved and rigged determines the outcome. Sloppy rigging and lousy presentation are snubbed. The trick is to make the quarry believe that what it sees and smells is worth the snacking.

Sorry, It's a TV Dinner: Frozen Fare

That brings us to the low end of the menu for shark vittles. In a pinch, following days of bad weather when it's been impossible to procure live or fresh fixin's, one must resort to the old box-of-frozen-bait trick. Whether it's mackerel, butterfish, menhaden, or herring, frozen and thawed baits will catch sharks; but they won't catch the persnickety ones. Most boxes of frozen bait will fit into a large cooler. Cover the cardboard box with seawater the evening before a sharking trip or first thing that morning, and the baits should thaw by the time you reach the fishing grounds.

Freezing baits causes a molecular change in their blood and flesh, so they don't draw strikes like the fresh stuff does. Frozen bait just doesn't smell or taste exactly right to the fussy eater, and is often snubbed. Still, we've caught a lot of fish with frozen TV dinners; sometimes it's the only option. A stock of frozen baits can make the difference between going sharking and chafing the dock.

Rigging Live Baits

Live-baiting for sharks was practiced around the turn of the century, and then revived in California and also along the

For small to medium sharks in the North Atlantic, a live menhaden can be fished on light tackle. The hook position allows the bait to swim deep.

South Coast of England during the past two decades. In the 1980s live-baiting moved into New England, and in the future freelining and trolling live ones will mean catches of active sharks that won't hit carrion.

While we can't discuss every method of rigging, we can show a few of the best proven arrangements for live-bait drifting or trolling. Live baits are easy to rig, and grounded in ways to keep the baitfish uninjured. We want the bait to remain active for an hour or more before being replaced with a livelier specimen.

One of the easiest ways to hook live bait is to pass the hook through the back, just to the rear of the dorsal fin. Make sure the hook isn't so deep that it hits the back-bone, or so shallow that it pulls out when the bait gets frisky. This post-dorsal method works well on various baitfish as long as the hook isn't too large, impeding the bait's movements or injuring it. Scad and mackerel fish well with this arrangement. And it works best when you're drifting on calm days and slack tides.

Perhaps the most positive way to rig a livey was perfected by Captain Ted Legg for porbeagles on the Isle of Wight grounds. It works well for thresher and mackerel sharks too. Ted passes the hook through the flesh near the bait's tail, then pins the hook under the skin just above the rib cage. With the hook in this central location, Ted's hookup rate averages a high 90 percent. For aggressive sharks he keeps his reels in gear, with a strike drag of 25 percent of line strength.

Hooks may also be placed through the lower and upper jaw or through the nostrils. These hook positions don't allow the bait to swim as deep as the Legg rig, but they work well on windy days and in rushing tides, when post-dorsal and Legg rigs may spin. Through-jaw live baits are popular in California, trolled in conjunction with a skirt or Baitmaster lure.

If you're using heavy tackle, big baits, and large hooks, rig a **through-eye yoke**. Guide a length of dental floss or old Dacron through the eye socket using a small bait needle. Knot the Dacron tight over the bait's head, then tie the larger hook in place, point up, with a couple of overhand knots and trim. This will keep any live bait in good condition for a lengthy drift or for slow-trolling. It's important to drift and troll active live baits. When a baitfish becomes docile, tie on a fresh one. Active sharks like porbeagles, makos, and threshers home in on the distress signals of a freshly hooked bait.

The Baitmaster and Bally-Hood

Live baits hooked through the lips or eye socket can be slow-trolled on a Baitmaster rig. This lure has a weighty swimming head and long vinyl skirt; the leader is through-wired with a hook hidden in the skirt. It can also be rigged with a swiveling hook or a stinger.

In California this live-bait and lure combo has accounted for good catches of makos and threshers. The Baitmaster, used with a live mack, is particularly good for threshers. It also works well with a mackerel strip bait, and will even take fish without any bait at all. For Baitmaster strip baits or slabs, use a fillet from a freshly killed mackerel to give lifelike color, and remove the tail. Good

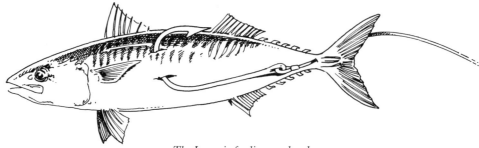

The Legg rig for live mackerel.

Mike "The Beak" Hurt

The Bally-Hood is a popular trolling aid, taking a live or fresh mackerel deep for makos and threshers.

skirt colors are green/white and red/yellow.

Similar devices include the Bait-O-Matic, much like the Baitmaster, and the Bally-Hood, which is available in several sizes. Basically, a live mackerel's head is tucked into the Bally-Hood's hood and impaled—sort of like The Bait without a Face, or The Bait with Excedrin Headache #223. Those who feel that this is cruel and unusual punishment can use baitfish freshly expired of natural causes.

Rigging Dead Baits for Chumming and Trolling

With a bit of rigging, fresh and frozen baits can look almost alive, especially when slow-trolled. You'll need a few rigging aids, such as **bait needles** (large darning needles work well), the ever-present **stockman's pliers**, a handy **fillet/rigging knife**, and **heavy dental floss** or the even-heavier **rigging thread**. It's also handy to have in your tackle locker a few egg sinkers from 6 to 16 ounces, brightly colored **plastic trolling skirts**, and various **rubber bands**. The egg sinkers and skirts can be slipped over the nose of any rigged bait to add extra appeal and weight for deep-trolling.

The easiest method of serving a dead bait is to push a hook through the bait's shoulder (in the back, just to the rear of the head). That's it. The bait will ride upright during a calm bluebird-day drift.

Another easy rig employs a fillet from a baitfish, such as a mackerel, bonito, or bluefish. Cut the fillet from the backbone, skin on, and push a hook through the skin so that the point will be on the flesh side. Fillets or "slabs" used in drifting and casting can be made more effective with a small amount of "Glow Bait" added to the fleshy side to lend a recently killed look. A standard fillet can become an appetizing sandwich with the addition of a whole squid; this can be very effective if twitched when a shark is spotted in its vicinity. You can also add a rear stinger hook to a lone fillet for normal drifting and subsurface trolling.

The **offset body rig** can be used in drifting or trolling, and its hook point stands away from the bait. The extra crimp it requires and the optional plastic skirt are passed onto the cable leader before an offset hook is attached. Push the hook through the bait's mouth and out through the gill slit. Halfway down the body, reverse the hook and push it into the flesh where the back meets the rib cage. A pull of the leader will let the hook face forward, the point sticking out and away from the bait's body. A rubber band will help keep the hook in place.

Next, lay the bait flat, leader tight, and slide the crimp down to the bait's nose. With a crimping tool, crimp the sleeve just enough to press it in place. Sew the jaw and nose shut with a rigging needle and floss, secure the floss to the crimp, and trim. The plastic skirt can now slide down over the crimp and tied floss, hiding the connection and giving the bait a colorful appeal. You can put an offset body rig together in less time than it takes to read these instructions. The crimp keeps the bait's body from sliding down the leader and forming a curve that can make the rig spin. For deeptrolling, add a 12- to 16-ounce egg sinker under the skirt and before the crimp.

The **throat rig** is another method of keeping a bait stationary on the leader so that it can be surface-trolled or drifted. After haywiring a hook to the leader, leave a short 6-inch tag sticking upright from the twist. Push the hook through the bait's throat so that you can push the tag up through the bait's lower jaw and nose. Bring the tag down to the main leader, finish off with four barrel wraps, and break it clean.

Here's an age-old method of fooling short strikers, the **internal stinger rig**. We call it the "Frankenstein bait" because it's finished with a sewing job only a monster could appreciate. Cut a slit in the bait's belly from the vent to the point where the ventral fins meet at the throat, and remove the entrails. Lay a preleadered primary hook at the forward point, where the bend of the hook will fetch against the throat. Rig a second hook on a short length of wire, and attach it to the eye of the forward hook so

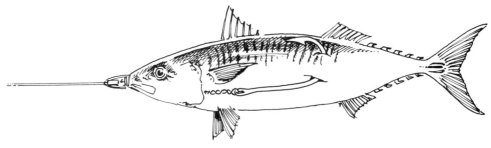

Offset body rig.

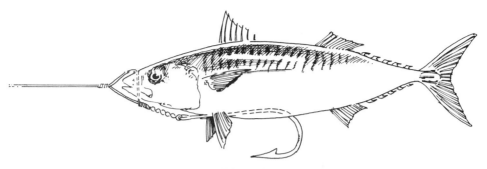

Throat rig.

that the secondary hook lies back at the vent.

Feed the leader of the primary hook out through the bait's mouth, and sew shut through chin, hook-eye, and nose. Place the short-leadered secondary hook inside the cavity. Starting at the throat, sew the cavity all the way to the vent and back up toward the throat, forming the classic X-shaped Frankenstein stitches, and tie the thread off. The finished bait can be towed or drifted. Although it takes a bit of work to get it right, it's excellent for sharks that short-hit the lower half of the bait. Charter customers marvel at this bait. Someday we'll jam a bolt and nut through the bait's head for that authentic touch.

A similar **external stinger rig** is used on the West Coast: a two-hook arrangement fashioned on 49-strand cable. The upper hook is pushed through the chin and nose of a live or dead mack or scad, and the lower hook is placed low and just forward of the tail, as in the offset body rig. It works well for deep-trolling and drifting, often spiced with an egg sinker under a bright green or red skirt.

The **simple chin rig**, for surface baits only, entails cutting a hole between the base of the bait's ventral fins and sliding a hook, eye first, back into the mouth until the eye reaches just inside the tip of the jaw and nose. Push the leader wire down through the nose, through the hook-eye, and through the lower jaw. Then press the leader and its tag tightly forward of the nose and jaw, closing the mouth, and wrap in a haywire twist.

The **weighted chin rig** is used exclusively in slow-trolling for large sharks that will take the entire bait in one bite, either

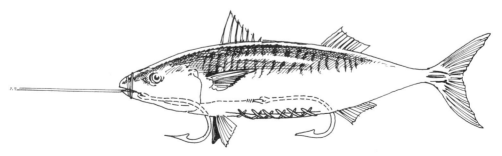

Frankenstein bait.

from a flat line, an outrigger, or a downrigger. Place the hook in the bait exactly as you would with the simple chin rig, with leader wire passing down through the nose and the hook-eye and out the chin area. Then slide an 8-ounce egg sinker on the tag end. Press the egg sinker against the chin as you form the haywire twist, and trim.

In the water, the weighted chin rig looks very realistic as it is trolled along; you can adjust the boat's speed to get a perfect, slow swim. If the rigged bait doesn't swim upright and naturally, opt for a heavier sinker. For short-strikers, you can add a stinger hook.

A Deboned Bait

To add further realism, debone a bait before rigging it weighted-chin style. Most saltwater tackle shops sell **deboning tools**

at a nominal price. Neatly removing a bait's backbone takes a little practice, but the result is amazing. The bait *actually swims,* tail wagging, just like a live offering.

Start the notched end of a deboning tool into the baitfish's backbone, either through the gill opening or through the mouth. Twist the tool back and forth when you find the "hard spot," where the backbone meets the head. Keep twisting with gentle pressure, and you'll feel the backbone break as the tool cuts through. Now angle the tool to run down the backbone, rotating in one direction only and snapping the ribs while you work down toward the tail.

Just before reaching the tail, stop rotating. Without puncturing the bait's skin, fold the tail back and forth to break the anterior portion of the backbone. While twisting the tool side to side, pull it back out of the fish. If all goes well, the backbone

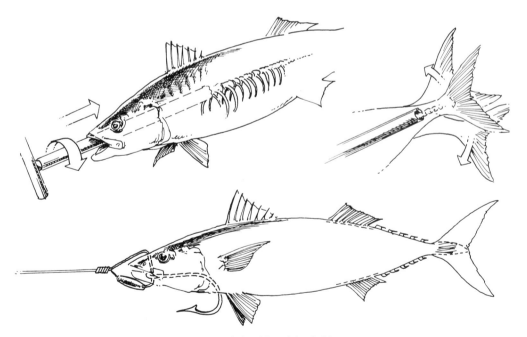

Deboned bait with weighted chin.

A deboning tool can be made from an 11-inch length of 7/16-inch I.D. stainless tubing, filed to a deep V-shaped notch at the cutting end. Make the notch with a triangular file.

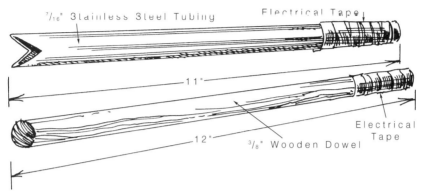

To remove the bait's backbone from the tool, make a "ramrod" from a 12-inch piece of 3/8-inch wooden dowel. For ease in handling, wrap a finger grip on the end of the tubing and dowel with plastic electrical tape. Use a hacksaw to cut dowel and tubing to length.

should remain inside the tubing; you can push it out with the dowel and discard it. The bait should look natural, although it will be very limp. Next, proceed with the weighted chin rig already described.

Natural baits and artificials presented under tow are new concepts in an old fishery. We have given an overview of several popular bait species, where and how to catch them, and how to rig them. Remember: a bait needn't be large to catch a trophy-size shark. Some species, like threshers, have a small mouth for their size and normally feed on bite-size prey. With a selection of baits of various sizes in our livewell and cooler, we're ready to go sharking.

6 CHUMMING

Peanut Pepper entices large sharks with fresh mackerel chunks. The sparkle of a chunk as it rolls down into the depths will often induce fish to feed.

AND TROLLING

It's a clear morning with a whisper of a breeze from the southwest; the seas will be like glass. The skipper will take us to a spot where this wind direction should work in our favor. We'll try the two most popular methods of sharking today: a good deal of chumming, or Rubby Dubby as they say in Britain, and a little bit of trolling.

Setting Up the Drift

A three-quarter-hour run brings us to an underwater mountain chain that peaks on our depth machine at 20 fathoms, or 120 feet. Between the submerged peaks, the depths run down to 50 fathoms. Indeed, local fishermen call this spot The Wall because of the steep contour of the eastern drop-off. The jagged bottom harbors a myriad of pelagic bait species, benthic fish, and the sharks that feed upon both. From Scotland to Australia the ocean is loaded with such coastal spots; remember, two-thirds of the world's mountains are under water.

Beyond The Wall, the ocean floor drops off to the east as a flat mud bottom, consistently remaining at about 56 to 58 fathoms. Today, the prevailing sou'westerly wind is less than 10 knots, and a running tide is rolling in from the south-southeast. Noting the wind and tide, the skipper figures the boat will drift to the north-northeast. He positions the boat at the break of the hard and the mud bottom, hoping that the combination of wind and tide will carry the boat along the edge or slightly up onto The Wall (see illustration, page 70).

The surface seawater temperature reads 62°F (17°C)—a little cold for makos, a little warm for porbeagles, but fine for blue sharks. We've seen bird activity and schools of baitfish at the surface—both good omens. As the engines shut down, we drop the chum crate overboard and ready the tackle, belts and harnesses, gaffs, and tagging stick.

Chumming: A Slick Operation

In the old days, shark fishermen ladled a soupy mixture of **ground chum** overboard.

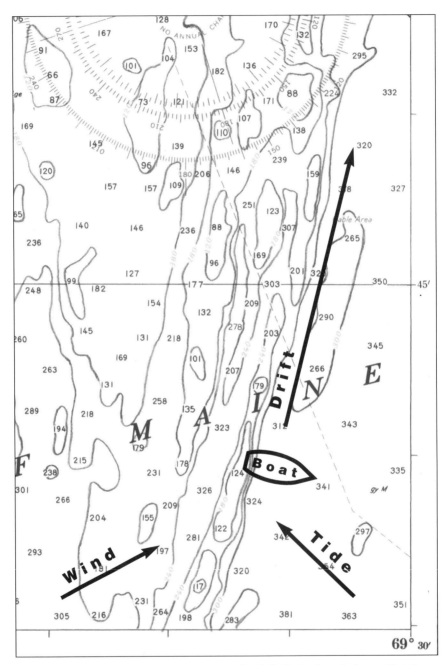

A good combination of wind and tide can aid a drift. Notice how the boat will drift along the edge of structure, where an abundance of sea life will be found.

When one ladleful disappeared into the depths, they dribbled another into the oily slick, as sun-baked chunks of rotting chum stuck to the rail and outer hull. Those days are gone, and we now depend on **frozen chum** hung over the side and in the water—where it belongs—in a heavy-duty chum bag, a plastic storage container, or a milk crate. The milk crate is the strongest of the three (see sidebar on page 74).

As we drift across the flat sea, 5 gallons of frozen bunker thaws in the crate, and small bits of chum sink slowly toward bottom. Many sharkers hang the chum crate from the bow or leeward side of the cockpit; but when a crate is so positioned, a shark approaching from underneath the boat may go undetected. We prefer to hang the crate on the windward side of the cockpit quarter, where we'll have a better view of any sharks approaching the chum ball.

In Calm Seas and Heavy Weather

The weather radio had forecast a calm day, so about half an hour before we left the marina, we dropped our bucket of frozen chum overboard to start thawing. Upon reaching the shark grounds, we removed the top of the chum bucket, slipped the crate down over it, inverted the bucket and crate, and lifted the bucket away from the partially frozen chum.

In today's calm seas, the mass of chum in the crate will leach better without the bucket. And a good slick is paramount to successful chumming. On flat days sharkers often lift the crate and slap it back down into the water to help start the slick.

In rough seas we leave the bucket in the crate to help protect the chum ball from heavy waves and keep the frozen chum from breaking up too fast. With these two methods of adapting to calm or rough water conditions, 5 gallons of frozen chum should last five or six hours.

Whenever possible, drift for offshore sharks, even when it's a little uncomfortable in winds of 15 to 20 knots. Drifting works best because it allows tactical freedom directly after a fish is hooked. If you must anchor, rig a poly-ball to the rode so you can cast it off if you need to maneuver the boat to follow a fish.

Anchors are a necessity for inshore sharking in tidal bays and river mouths. Position your boat upcurrent, allowing the tide to carry the chum slick down over a drop-off, where sharks may lurk in the depths. When you anchor in a river mouth, stay clear of the navigational channel and the large boats using it.

And steer clear of anchoring along the edges of coral reefs. Anchors destroy the living coral, so please find another spot to fish, such as a nearby wreck. Or drift along the edges of the reef, using a sea anchor to help hold position.

A parachute-style sea anchor also can be used offshore on windy days to slow down a drift. The better ones are equipped with a trip line so that they can be hauled aboard quickly. Depending on the direction of the chum slick, the sea anchor can be secured to a cleat farther aft than the standard bow chock, so baits drift in the lane.

Positioning the Baits

As the chum slick starts to smooth out the ocean's surface, we set out three baits, each positioned at a different depth. The first bait, usually a large whole mackerel or a substantial fillet, will be positioned about 100 feet away from the boat, about 10 to 15

Light
Rig

Single
Wire
Leader

Live
Bait

fathoms deep. In a running tide, this bait may require additional weight to keep it down, so we wrap an 8-ounce bank sinker to the wire leader, about a foot below the swivel, with a breakaway rubber band.

To keep this outer bait's line high and to decrease the chances that it will tangle with the second bait during the drift, we usually attach the bait line to an outrigger clip and run it up to the top of the rigger (left in the upright position). The clip is adjusted to open under a light pull, so that the line will pop free when a shark picks up the bait.

The second bait, a live one if possible, can be positioned about 60 feet from the boat at a depth of 5 to 7 fathoms. Usually, no additional weight is needed. These two outer baits are held to a specific depth by inflated **balloons** attached directly to the line with a single overhand knot. Another method for attaching the balloon employs a 2-foot section of light line running from the balloon to a small rubber band, and pulled through itself several times around the main line. This is a preferred method for shark species that like to play with balloons.

Some sharkers use chunks of Styrofoam as floats, but we consider this an envi-ronmentally destructive material. Oval Styrofoam floats, often carried by dealers who sell sharking tackle, can be safely attached in-line. Wrap a heavy rubber band around the float a couple of times, slide the float up the main line, and attach the swivel. At the required depth for the bait, loop the main line under the rubber band to hold it in place. This float will remain in-line and can be reset over and over on the two outer rigs.

Our third bait, often a smaller live or dead fish, is dunked right at boat-side without a float. We like to keep it in sight so we can actually spot the shark grab it. The depth depends on water clarity, which can vary from 25 or 30 feet in blue water to less than 20 feet in green water.

Since you'll be unable to identify size or species on the two outer baits, rig them to medium-heavy, 50-lb tackle. The close positioning of the third bait, usually rigged to a 30-lb outfit, allows a judgment call before the fish takes. If, for example, the shark turns out to be a massive mako, yarn the bait into the cockpit and replace it by reeling one of the outside baits into position.

On the other hand, if the fish is a 5-foot

blue shark, take it on the bait offered, or try for it with even lighter tackle. We keep a rigged light-tackle outfit handy in the cockpit, leader attached, with the bait on ice.

There are funky days when contrary winds and tide send a slick one way and your baits another, but there are ways around this. If the baits are running off the stern quarter and the chum is slicking in toward the bow, try placing a **flatline clip** (or clothespin attached to a line) on the bow rail. Attach the bait line to this clip, and chances are the bait will swing back into the slick.

Bait positioning is flexible anyway. We fish our baits closer to the boat than some sharkers do because we think it's easier to set the hook that way. If there's a good breeze or ripping tide, you may need additional weight and depth below the float. Some sharkers like to hang a very deep bait directly under the boat, just above bottom structure or the thermocline, which appears as a distinct line when the gain is increased on most depth recorders. Anglers who fish the depths use a heavier rod and reel because their bait is deep into the unknown. No matter where baits are placed, use no more than three, and check them often for tangles and washouts.

Sharks in the Slick

A chum slick can start to work immediately, or it can take hours to toll a shark to the

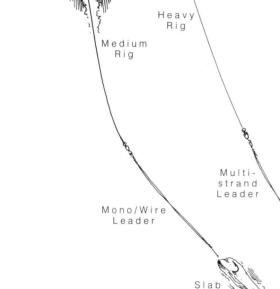

Heavy
Rig

Medium
Rig

Multi-
strand
Leader

Mono/Wire
Leader

Slab
Bait

Stinger
Bait

*Drifting three different rigs
in a chum slick.*

Rigging the Super Bucket

This modification to the milk crate makes chumming much easier. To contain the chum in the crate, add a rugged "bait bag" knitted from 6-thread commercial pot warp. Coat the netter's knots with Pliobond for stability. Gather the loops of the mesh and pass a line, about 7 feet long, through them; tie off with a couple of overhand knots. Clove-hitch a 40-inch poly-ball to the line about 2 feet from the bucket.

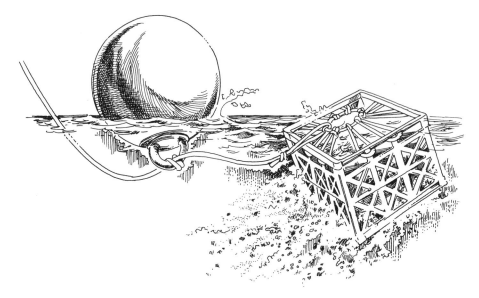

Drop the chum-packed Super Bucket and poly-ball overboard, pass the line down through the stern chock, and fasten it to a cleat. When you hook a shark, start the engines and cast the bucket free. As you maneuver the boat during the fight, the chum will remain in the slick, chumming away. After the shark has been caught and released, run back to the chum slick, retrieve the bucket by gaffing the line between the crate and the poly-ball, and set out your shark baits again. The Super Bucket is easy to use, and turns a once nasty job into an enjoyable one.

baits. Usually, the slick will produce a fish in about an hour, but we have drifted over productive bottom for many hours without so much as a nibble. Check the depth recorder often to make sure the boat is drifting over submerged peaks and not over a flat mud bottom. If a drift turns sour and the water seems lifeless, consider moving to a more productive spot—but don't be *too* hasty: It may be coincidence, but many long, unproductive drifts hold an ultimate prize. We have often drifted for hours without sighting the expected blue sharks, only to have a mako turn up in the slick. In each instance, however, the depth machine showed us over productive bottom, with cod and baitfish deep in the water column.

How long it takes to toll in the first bite depends on how deep the sharks are. If they're deep, it will take time to attract them to the surface. Usually. On one occasion the fish were so close to the surface that we had a hookup immediately upon setting out the first bait. Unfortunately, the anglers, a family from Ohio, succumbed to mal-de-mer. We caught the shark, tagged it, and struck out for home. All told, we logged three hours of running time and 10 minutes of fishing.

Sharks always zigzag up through the chum slick. Guided by their keen olfactories, the fish swim in a long, continuous S-curve—intersecting the chum line, passing beyond it, then coming back in again. If they're approaching on the surface, you can spot them at a distance, not only in the slick but well out to the left and right of it.

You won't notice a shark approaching from the depths until a balloon dances or suddenly disappears under water and the clicker starts screaming. On calm days sharkers generally keep reels in **free-spool, clicker on,** so that the fish feels no resistance as it takes the bait. On windy days and during running tides, you may need to move the reel lever forward just enough to engage the gears so the bait doesn't pull line from the reel spool.

If a shark strikes quickly and line starts screaming off the reel, pick up the rod, slip the reel into gear or *strike*, and set the hook. Slow takes require a little more judgment—

"The slower the take, the longer the wait." But if we wait too long, three things can happen: The fish could accidentally prick itself and drop the bait; it could swallow the bait to its stomach; or it could continue up the slick and grab a second bait.

Aggressive sharks like porbeagles and threshers are sometimes live-baited with the reel in gear. Captain Ted Legg, who fishes out of Portsmouth, England, favors taking both species with the reel set at the strike position during the drift, with the hook located at the center of the live bait. Not only did this raise Ted's hookup rate but "There was an additional bonus from this technique. Sharks were always hooked around the jawbone at the side of the mouth. This resulted in a better fight from the sharks and also enabled me to remove the hooks prior to release alongside the boat." From his *Kittywake*, Captain Legg has had record success.

At times, a slick will attract so many sharks that it's impossible to use three rods. We have looked back at the chum ball while fighting a fish and watched two or three more sharks chewing at the crate and slapping the poly-ball with their tails. After releasing the shark, we jogged back to the poly-ball, slipped the engines into neutral, and dropped a single bait to the waiting fish.

Oh No, It's Running under the Boat!

Successful anglers know that it pays to lead a hooked shark well away from the poly-ball whether it's drifting with the chum crate or attached to an anchor. Light lines will chafe and break in seconds after running against an anchor line or the boat's hull. Often, it's the really prized fish that pulls this trick.

Requiem sharks (such as the blue whaler), more so than mackerel sharks, usually feed by smell. Often they are the first fish to show up in the chum line.

The classic punishment that fish inflict upon anglers is the old run-under-the-boat trick. This happens all too often, especially when a shark is played from a dead boat; it accounts for most lost sharks. The only way to deal with this situation requires quick action: three moves are performed in just a few seconds.

When it becomes apparent that the shark will pass under the boat, put the reel in free-spool, or in the case of a star drag, flip the reel lever into free-spool to remove tension from the line. At the same time, thumb the spool to avoid an overrun. As quickly as possible, unsnap the harness (if one is used) from the reel lugs and pop the gimbal out of the rod belt.

Now lean over the side of the boat, submerging the rod vertically to within a few inches of the reel. While the fish takes line, walk the rod around the stern until the line clears the hull, rudders, and propellers. Then lift the rod from the water, reset the drag, and continue playing the fish.

It takes a bit of practice to perfect this whole procedure, and it's much easier without a harness. Some harnesses, however, can be modified to use "French clips," which allow rod removal in seconds.

Teasing with Chunks

Some fish come up through the slick and pass right by every bait. They may swim curiously around the boat or even start biting the chum crate. These fish were imprinted on small pieces of chum in the slick, and they're now feeding on bits, not baits. You can still catch them though.

One method is to offer the shark a freshly hooked live bait. If that doesn't work, give it what it really wants. Pull a baitfish from the cooler and cut it into small chunks, tossing a few chunks at the shark to check its reaction. If the fish eats them, give it a chunk with a hook buried in it.

Chunking is a very effective method of teasing all species of sharks, and many sharkers augment their chum line this way. Some anglers do a bit of minichunking when they start the chum line—a way to augment the initially slow thawing of the frozen ball. Other sharkers chunk during the entire drift, believing that the silvery flash of chunks induces sharks to feed. Be careful not to overchunk: A shark full of chunks is through feeding until it digests its meal. And sharks (except makos) digest their meals very slowly.

Tolling Mackerel Sharks

All mackerel sharks are tuned to the distress signals of baitfish, particularly bottom fish hooked on rod and reel. British anglers have noted that porbeagles are drawn to a constant stream of caught and released baitfish. Scottish anglers regularly practice "feathering" on the shark "marks" (grounds), catching hundreds of macks or cod and releasing them as sonic attractors.

The same activity aboard Gulf of Maine headboats will draw makos and porbeagles to the surface. Often we jig for cod

Although not an easy maneuver, dipping the rod and swinging around the stern is the only way to save a fish that has run under the boat.

while drifting for sharks aboard the *Lucky Star II;* and on good jerking days, when many small cod are hooked and released, a large mackerel shark will rise to the boat. The trick, of course, is to avoid hooking the mako on the cod rod, which culminates in a short and silly fight that the mako always wins. Deeper live baits suspended along the jerking lane may be the answer. The technique is new, but the result may be a substantial increase in porbeagle and mako catches where these two species are known to exist but have been difficult to entice.

Trolling
for Teeth

The art of chumming and chunking takes a little practice. Nobody can learn what's too much or too little in the first few outings. But it's worth the effort to learn because these methods have produced the vast majority of requiem sharks caught within the sport. Slow-trolling, borrowing techniques from tuna and bill fishermen, is a very distant second, perhaps because it's relatively new for sharks.

Subsurface, or blind, trolling can be exciting because you never know what creature will hit the bait. You may hook a tuna anywhere from New Jersey waters north to the Gulf of Maine, so consider heavy gear when using weighted rigs.

Trolling
the Surface

Heading to and from the shark grounds, we often see sharks finning along on the surface. They're usually blue sharks, but other species, too, will fin in the sun's rays, including makos, porbeagles, and threshers.

On one occasion, aboard Tom McFall's *Galadriel,* a sighted basking shark turned out to be, upon closer inspection, a great white. Since all sharks like to bask, keep a keen eye out for these telltale finners.

Upon sighting a finning fish, we slow down to 3 or 4 knots, attach a surface bait to a lowered outrigger, and tow it well astern, about 200 feet behind the transom. We match our gear to the estimated size of the fish, and set the reel's lever drag so that it just barely keeps line from leaving the spool. Before slipping the engines into neutral, the skipper steers the boat well ahead of the finner so that the bait will intersect its path about 20 feet ahead of the fish.

The bait will now slowly sink, and the shark will turn or slip beneath the surface if it wants the bait. When the trolling line pops from the outrigger, throw the reel into free-spool, clicker on, and let the shark mouth the bait just as with chumming.

This style of surface trolling was used many decades ago for swordfish off Montauk, Nantucket, Nova Scotia, and Chile. In the future, surface-trolling sharkers may borrow the kite from bill fishermen. This would allow us to sneak up on spooky fish that are shy of engine noise. Taking sharks by surface trolling is just more fun than chumming; no doubt Captain George Farnsworth's kite and other established gamefish techniques will slide into the sharker's bag of tricks for those calm, sunny days when there's a lot of topwater activity.

Subsurface Techniques

On days when finning sharks are few, a spread of trolled surface and deep baits may do the trick. While looking for finning fish, you can troll a subsurface chin-weighted bait down the middle and well behind two out-

Barry Gibson

One of the first East Coast sharks taken on a trolled bait, this porbeagle
fell to a chin-rigged mackerel.

rigger surface baits, or tow it about 30 to 40 feet deep behind a downrigger ball. The sub-surface bait may catch the attention of sharks cruising too deep to be seen.

Anglers may elect to slow-troll an entire subsurface selection, a practice gaining popularity in California waters for makos and threshers. Whenever you're deep-trolling, add another stinger or trailer hook to the baits. Makos and many other sharks tend to bite the rear of a baitfish to immobilize it, then circle around and eat the rest. With a stinger, you can usually set the hook on the initial strike.

A typical subsurface layout includes a very deep bait towed at a depth of 60 to 100 feet on a downrigger, a second bait fished flatline style, and a third bait fished from an outrigger. Adjust the lever drags to just under the strike position, with the clicker on to act as a warning. When a shark hits, pop up to full *strike* and set the hook.

When fishing a full complement of deep-trolled baits, anglers can present the fish with a smorgasbord. The downrigger bait can be a whole fish rigged with a plastic skirt over its head, or it can be a mackerel fillet. A bait towed from the outrigger could be another skirted whole fish with a heavy (12- to 16-ounce) egg sinker hidden beneath the skirt; or it could be a weighted chin-rigged natural. And the flat line could drag either style of rigged whole bait fished shorter than the rigger lines.

On the West Coast slow-trolling has been very successful with makos and threshers. Some Californians use dual downriggers, dropping the two baits to different depths, perhaps towing one down near the thermocline and another live bait closer to the surface.

California's Dave Elm, a knowledgeable thresher angler and thermocline

bumper, actually prefers trolling to drifting and chumming. "I believe the larger, more aggressive sharks tend to attack a slow-trolled bait better. Also, by slow-trolling you cover more ground, pulling baits through more of the water column. When trolling, I always use two downriggers, one at 130 feet and the other at 75 feet. Then down the center I put the Baitmaster."

These West Coast catches of makos and threshers on downriggers prove further that deep-trolling works with sharks. A few years back, Captain Barry Gibson's old *Shark II* landed one of the first mackerel

Mike "The Beak" Hurt

The Baitmaster is the most popular artificial-natural rig for active sharks. Shown with a stinger hook and slab.

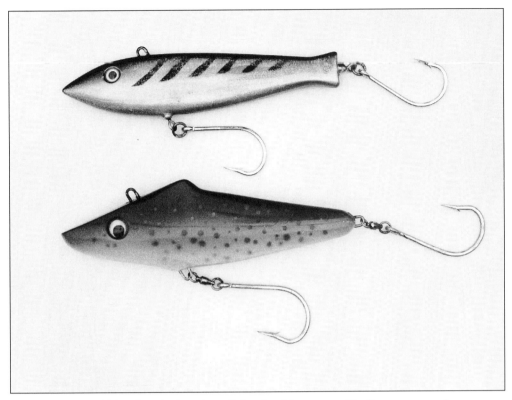

The Braid Speedster (top) can be trolled at 6 to 8 knots, yet will still attract aggressive sharks. The Magnum Flash Dancer (bottom) is effective down to 4 knots.

sharks taken on the East Coast by subsurface trolling. Last season alone several dozen blue sharks were taken by this method in New England waters, so it's worth the effort to try similar techniques in your own local seas.

Deep-Trolling Artificials

Californians are also adding artificial lures to their subsurface spread of skirted naturals and Baitmaster rigs. The heavy metal lures, made by Dennis Braid and equipped with two double hooks, bring to mind a giant version of the old Coastal Jig. Braid's

impressive "Predator" model weighs in at 20 ounces, much heavier than previous similar offerings like the original Cairns Swimmer. Dennis's "Flash Dancer" has also taken its share of makos and threshers, and is a favorite of Captain Beak Hurt.

The most popular mako color is Braid's "Green Mack," often towed flatline style, about 60 or 70 feet directly behind the boat, with a medium trolling outfit. For these lures, the reel is set at *strike*. There's no doubt that these new lures are taking aggressive sharks.

In light of the recent successes by Dennis, Captain "Bongo Joe" Bairian, and

"The Beak," anglers fishing in areas thick with makos and threshers should give this method a try. Lures with a similar action and color—such as the Cairns Swimmer, the Marauder, and the new Australian Runner—may be effective on smaller mackerel sharks. And towed from a downrigger, these solid-plastic lures will track deeper than they would fished from a flat line.

No matter the style of presentation—totally artificial, a Baitmaster combo, or a plain chin-rigged mackerel—the best slow-trolling speeds are from 3 to 5 knots. Surface trolling works best at lower speeds, giving the bait just enough momentum to remain on top. Deepwater speeds are most effective at the high end—fast enough for the natural-artificial combos to work correctly. You may need to fine-tune the boat's speed when trolling into or away from a current or the wind.

Troll over the best ground available, keeping one eye on the depth recorder and the other on the surface. If the machine shows a large mark, which could be a shark above or below the range of the baits, adjust them to tow at the mark's depth. East Coast trollers should use heavy gear—50- or 80-lb

Mike "The Beak" Hurt

Don't let anyone say that sharks are stupid; they're smart enough to avoid hooks and to figure out how to do it.

outfits—because the eventual bite may come from a monster. West Coast sharkers usually troll with gear one or two sizes lighter.

Trolling for sharks as for other species, such as tuna and billfish—has a higher hookup rate than chumming or chunking, and you can cover more water in the same amount of time. Also, more fish survive trolling since most are hooked in the corner of the mouth. Remember that the regime works best in areas that have a concentration of aggressive sharks, and experiment by trolling baits at various depths.

Bowling for Sharks

Our Maine friend John Shostak, a local tuna and shark fisherman, takes bold surface-cruising fish with a wicked-odd technique that he calls "bowling for sharks." Approaching the finning animal at idle, John actually throws a bait at the fish by the same underhand toss bowlers use. It isn't exactly "trolling" in the true sense of the word, but it works, and it's a lot of fun. And that's what sharking is all about.

LIGHT

Mark Sosin

On the flats, an artificial lure is often retrieved as a "crippled minnow." This lemon shark is interested and starts to charge the plug.

TACKLE
SHARKING

Sharks have proven themselves to be exciting and sometimes explosive adversaries on light tackle. Whether an angler prefers the mysteries of the deep or the shallows of a tropical flat, there is a set of jaws appropriate for threadlining. Blue sharks, tope, small makos, blacktips, spinners, leopards, and lemons are all potential game for the angler wielding a spinning, casting, or light "conventional" outfit.

If light-tackle angling appeals to you, the basic techniques described in the previous chapters will make a good starting point. The longer parabolic rods associated with light tackle are obvious departures from the stiff trolling and stand-up gear usually used in sharking and require different techniques (anglers can't use a short-stroke pump, for example), but the inherent elasticity of a casting or spinning rod does have a few advantages of its own. **Constant pressure**, the nemesis of all gamefish, can be readily applied; and providing that a light rod has enough **lifting power**, some very large sharks can be brought to boat-side. In using light tackle, we discover that thin, 12- to 20-lb test, or even lighter line,

offers a degree of enjoyment that exceeds our wildest expectations.

Spinning for Sharks

With a modicum of care and a little talent, **spinning outfits** can whip a shark of 100 pounds or less. Choose a 6½- to 7-foot rod designed for 1- to 3-ounce lures and lines up to 25-lb test. We recommend purchasing a rod made by a company that specializes in saltwater tackle, such as Penn, Shimano, Fenwick, Star, Cal-Star, Daiwa, or Loomis. The matching spinning reel should be a quality item, with a smooth drag and the capacity to spool at least 300 yards of 20-lb test line.

In the past, we have used the traditional Penn 704Z with success. Penn's newer Spinfisher SS6500 through 8500 sport improvements in line capacity over the older Z models. Some spinning reels, such as the Shimano BaitRunners and Silstar Bait Feeder series, have a free-spool lever for drifting and live-baiting. A great idea. Other good reels include the Abu Garcia GM7,

Quantum Blue Runner 3-60, and Daiwa BG60 or the larger BG90. All of these spinning models feature a front-mounted drag, a heavy-duty system ideal for sharks.

A spinning outfit may not be the best tool for active sharks, even though its popularity is entrenched in our sport. The basic design of a spinning reel creates a major problem for beginners. When the crank is turned while the line is paying out, the mono will twist once for every turn of the reel handle. If slack forms in the line, it twists back down over itself, knots, and pops.

Despite the few drawbacks to the spinning reel, many anglers have become threadline artists, taking trophy-size fish on monofilament rated at 2- and 4-lb test. Threadlining is not for everybody, but it has a core of itinerant devotees who have mastered their feel for the amount of pressure their lines can withstand. This is light-tackle angling at its lightest, and a smaller reel is fitted to a rod designed for 1-ounce—or even lighter—lures.

The ultralight spinning outfit is ideal for bonnetheads in the tropics and tope in temperate zones. Using the light wand, Elizabeth Feldman has taken impressive fish at Parengarenga Harbor in New Zealand, including a 36-pounder that was the 4-lb-class record until it was defeated by her daughter Melanie. Light-line tope battles are lengthy, often requiring hours of constant pressure on the fish—plenty of time for fatigue and mistakes. Hats off to the ladies' light touch.

Casting Tackle— An Alternative

Seasoned anglers who have advanced in the sport by using conventional (trolling or revolving-spool) outfits, often prefer **bait-casting tackle** over the spinning version, so they can pump the rod with the arm they've trained for lifting a conventional trolling rod.

Many newer anglers believe that a casting reel is difficult to master and that the resulting "bird's nests" from spool overrun are too much trouble. Today's casting reels are a far cry from the older models, and those made by Abu Garcia and Penn have practically licked the old "crow's nest" problem.

There are other advantages too: A casting outfit enables you to make longer and more accurate casts. You can adjust its drag system without getting "line burn." And it allows you to fish with your dominant hand at the reel.

Considering the extended durations and touchy situations involved in light-tackle shark fishing, it is a great asset to have an outfit designed exactly like the trolling or boat gear we normally use. Surprisingly, younger anglers find the miniconventional system is easier to use for bottom-fishing, especially if they haven't been conditioned to the spinning mode. Light freshwater-"bass"-style rods, with their abbreviated grip-length, seem to fit young bodies best; children can move up to heavier casting tackle as they grow.

In choosing standard casting tackle, opt for the same size range prescribed for spinning. The rod should have backbone, lifting power, and a tip strong enough to set a 4/0 to 8/0 O'Shaughnessy or Beak Claw hook in a shark's jaw. Our personal favorites are triggered models, often called *popping rods* and billed as "medium-heavy." Light-tackle sharker Abe Cuanang touts the 7-foot Fenwick Trigger Stick (STG 706M). Ambassadeur reels lead in pure castability, and the new Pro Max 6600W and 7500C are a pleasure. The Penn 980 Mag Power,

Lightlining for sharks often puts maximum pressure on fish and tackle. Rods built from E-glass, shown here, accomplish the task best.

Shimano 200FS, or Daiwa SL20SH reels are also excellent choices. All these reels cast easily (in the order listed) and have good drag systems.

With a little bit of practice on smaller species, it doesn't take long for an angler to become proficient with casting tackle. There is an inherent feel to a casting outfit that no other form of tackle can provide. For light-tackle sharking, it is a joy to use.

Whether you choose a spinning or casting outfit, you can do a great deal of light-line work without making a cast—simply by drifting or freelining baits or by weighting them to bottom. Benthic sharks are ideal targets for bottom-baiting, and they are all worthy coastal opponents. Offshore species like blue sharks and smaller makos will also accept a bait drifted in their feeding lane. Over tropical wrecks, anglers will discover that blacktip and lemon sharks can be chummed up to the same light tackle.

Light-Tackle Leaders

Any wire or mono/wire leader used for light-tackle work is basically a miniaturized

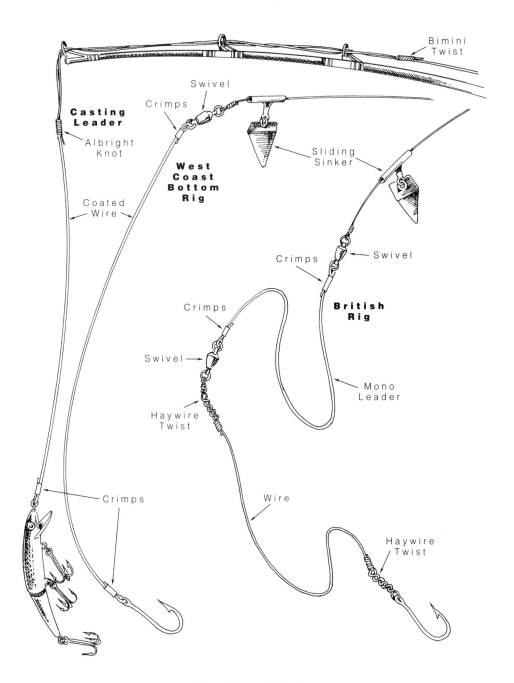

Bimini
Twist

Swivel

Crimps

**Casting
Leader**

Albright
Knot

**West
Coast
Bottom
Rig**

Sliding
Sinker

Coated
Wire

Crimps

Swivel

Crimps

**British
Rig**

Swivel

Mono
Leader

Haywire
Twist

Wire

Haywire
Twist

Crimps

Three light-tackle leaders.

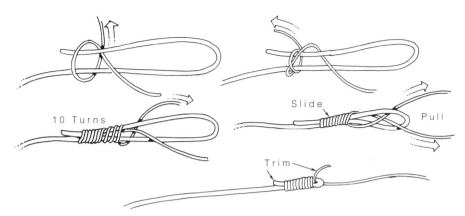

The Albright knot.

version of the rigs described earlier. Always double the last 2 feet of the monofilament casting line, with a Bimini twist, ahead of any light-tackle leader. For bottom species and bait-dunking, leaders can be fairly long.

Tope anglers often use a shortened and scaled-down version of the mono/wire leader system. Simon Williams, a very successful small-craft sharker in Wales, uses light tackle exclusively. "The trace," he comments, "consists of 12 to 15 inches of wire (60-lb test) connected to 4 to 5 feet of heavy mono (60- to 80-lb test) which is then tied to the main line by a swivel." Using this combo leader in shallow areas, tope specialists free-line a whole mackerel to bottom. In deeper water, over 25 feet, a sliding sleeve with a sinker (ledger rig) is employed.

This is similar to the coastal leader system used for leopard and soupfin sharks in California. Leopard rigs employ the running sleeve, sinker attached, on the main line, but the wire portion is made from coated 90-lb test multi-strand. The main line and hook are attached to the short leader by a barrel swivel and crimps, and the preferred bait is a midshipman.

Make sure that the running sleeve is

passed onto the main line before you tie the Bimini. If the knot enters the sleeve, use a small plastic bead as a stopper, or omit the double line and attach the single main line to the swivel with a Uniknot or improved clinch.

For actual casting, shorter leaders (3 feet or less) will make a toss more enjoyable. Most short casting leaders employ a section of heavy mono ahead of 12 to 15 inches of wire, either coated or single-strand. For bluewater work, tie a mono shocker to the Bimini with an **Albright knot** and attach a short section of #9 wire to a barrel swivel on the other end. On the flats, where sharks may spook, omit the barrel swivel and tie a nylon-coated leader directly to the doubled line with an Albright. Finish the arrangement by attaching the hook (or plug) with a figure-eight knot and/or crimp.

For casting bait in the shallows, slide a small egg sinker and plastic bead over the main line, giving just enough weight to make a 40- to 60-foot cast. Drop the baitwell ahead of a cruising shark's path, so that the splash of the rig won't spook it. When the shark picks up the offering, the line will slide through the egg sinker with little resistance. This rig can also be used to moderate depths, where sharks are a bit bolder.

Casting and Drifting to Pelagics

With a little practice, anglers can cast to surface-finning deep-water sharks by using a small bait hooked through the lower jaw and nose. The bait's skull is strong enough to keep it from flying off the hook during casting. Try to cast the bait about 10 feet ahead of the cruising fish, then open the spinning reel's bail or thumb the conventional model in *free-spool*, and feed the line to the shark through the fingers of your left hand. If the shark grabs the offering, allow it to mouth the bait for 5 to 10 seconds before you flip the bail and set the hook.

Deep-water sharks that are chummed to the boat are easier targets because anglers can get an accurate estimate of their size. During a normal day's drift, the perfect fish will often home in on the bait closest to the boat, usually our third bait (as described in "Positioning the Baits" in Chapter 6). Crank this bait in and replace it with the spinning rod's offering. If a stocked baitwell is handy, grab a small livey and slip a hook through the flesh of the fish just in back of the dorsal. Gently flip the bait in the direction of the shark; he'll find it quick enough.

Along the East Coast, blue sharks are common light-tackle targets, and they present one major problem: they tend to roll up the leader, touching the threadline and breaking off instantly. To compensate for the rolling of a blue shark, the boat handler should slip the engine into gear and try to position the boat just ahead of the running

fish. If the line is slightly ahead of the shark, the animal will have difficulty getting that first wrap of a roll. If the fish remains near the surface, where it can be fought visually, there's a good chance you'll get it. But if the blue shark sounds into the depths, you'll need some luck. The real trick is learning to **feel what the shark is doing.** Many light-wand advocates use one line rating exclusively, learning the maximum tolerance of the tackle.

West Coast sharkers have the opportunity to capture small makos on light tackle since there are many California makos in the 40- to 60-pound range, an ideal size for the light-tackle buff. Like blue

Joe Libby of the Breakaway *displays a small mako taken at dusk on spinning gear. The fish hit a well-placed Atom popper.*

sharks, makos present a tactical, albeit different, problem—they jump. And if they land on the threadliner's fragile monofilament, it will pop. But often you can avoid a broken line by **"bowing" to the fish,** an old trick used by light-tackle billfish and tarpon anglers. When the fish leaps into the sky, lean toward the mako and point the rod at it to put some slack in the line so that the line will be less likely to break if the fish falls on it. We know it's not polite to point, but the makos won't be offended.

Bottom-Bumping

Inshore sharking, practiced globally, is a very popular form of connecting with mid-size requiems and a few of their cousins. The targets—mostly coastal benthics—include school sharks, soupfins, leopards, and sandbar sharks. Except in some areas of Great Britain, most bottom-sharking is accomplished without the rote of "Rubby Dubby"—it's tidy shark angling. Whether beneath New Jersey's Mannisquam Bridge or in the channels of Cardigan Bay, Wales, this form of angling for temperate species is carried out at anchor.

Since most of the fishing is in protected waters, small skiffs and light trailerables are often used; and the boats locate and anchor over productive channel edges, holes, and shallow ridges. Anglers then drop baits to bottom, often in running tides. Weight will be needed, and most sinkers are snapped to a sliding T-shaped runner that allows the main line to slide easily through it. For light tackle, most anglers opt for standard pyramids.

Depending on the tide and the strength of the line, pyramid sinkers may vary from a few ounces to a half-pound. Choose a weight heavy enough to hold bot-

Angelo Cuanang used a bottom rig with a running pyramid sinker to hold ground for this light-tackle leopard.

tom so that the bait will not roll. There is a limit to the depth you can fish effectively with a light rod; when it's exceeded, your bait will be lifted from the bay's floor, useless. With an easy tide, it's possible to remain steady at 90 feet, but the usual limit is 50 to 60 feet.

Many bottom sharkers favor a sandwich approach to baiting: a fish chunk or fillet and a piece of squid. When the fish takes the bait, the angler leaves the reel out of gear and freelines the offering as the shark runs across bottom. When the fish stops to turn the bait in its mouth, most anglers pause for a few seconds before setting the hook.

If the shark is small, there's a good chance you can take it without hauling the anchor. With schooling sharks, like tope and soupfin, it's best to remain on location. If the bite gets heavy, several anglers can hook fish and do the Cross-Over Boogie. Occasionally, an outsized fish is tapped, and the anchor must be hauled. Small boats—under power or in tow—are often led across miles of water as the shark attempts a marathon getaway.

These long fights are a strain on light wands and the anglers who wield them. Arms tremble and fingers cramp into claws. Sometimes the overtaut line will actually sing in the breeze. Threadlined sharks are not regular bottom fish; capturing them requires stamina and perseverance.

Time, Tide, and Top Bait

Since extended bouts may continue for two to three hours, light-tackle anglers have learned that long periods of waiting for the bite cut down on quality time. They must learn when and where to find the greatest concentrations of the sharks they're after and find out what the biggest individuals are feeding on. Choose the optimum time of the season and tide. In Wales, for instance, schools of tope pass through local waters from May to September. The peak season, however, lasts from mid-June to mid-August—coinciding with the Atlantic mackerel run—so for the largest tope, a whole mack is used as bait. The time to connect is

when the tope are thick. Like most sharks, tope feed best on the running tide. Slack tide periods, dead high, and the end of the ebb often signal the end of their feeding periods.

In San Francisco Bay, which has a sizable population of leopard sharks and a few active soupfins thrown in for sport, the season lasts year-round. But the best time is the spring-tide period. That's when the midshipmen are most accessible, and the ugly little critters are fished live for the biggest leopards.

Those who regularly fish for active sharks in the Bay collect these 6-inch baits by turning over exposed rocks during the very low spring tides. Midshipmen are also available at some San Francisco–area tackle shops. They're fished along the channel edges at depths anywhere from 15 to 60 feet, and the best time is the last two hours before high tide.

Blue sharks are concentrated on the eastern and western coasts of the Atlantic at approximately the same time. The peak migration period is August, when there are packs of small individuals offshore for your light-tackle angling pleasure. This is also the time of calm seas and perfect light-tackle weather. On the California coast, suitable flat-seas weather arrives a month later. Again, running tides are best, and the top bait is a whole mackerel.

Makos are another story. They are never plentiful except in the waters of Southern California.

Blacktips and lemons are at their thickest off both coasts of South Florida. These sharks move up onto the flats from deeper waters as the tide rises. Here, they will feed for just a few hours; when the tide ebbs, they will move back out into deeper water. Check the local tide tables, and be there when the fish are. During the summer

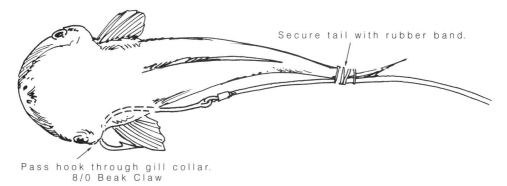

Secure tail with rubber band.

Pass hook through gill collar.
8/0 Beak Claw

Rigged midshipman bait (top view).

months, when water on the flats is its warmest, an angler will find the highest concentrations of toothy game.

Spinning and Casting on the Flats

Light-tackling the flats is probably the most intense form of sharking. It requires keen eyesight, muscle power on the rod, and hours in a baking sun. Yet the rewards for these trials can be the greatest ones. We admit our eye-balling technique suffers—we could spot a great deal more at age 20 than we can now at 50. But while we have trouble seeing the fish, we can still spot their activity.

There are a few tricks that can help the old eyeballs as you traverse a seemingly endless expanse of shallows. To minimize glare, try not to pole the skiff into the sun. Pick an area ahead that has dark clouds, and wear polarized sunglasses and a wide-brimmed hat. And be as quiet as humanly possible; that goes for talking, too. Be a regular Whispering Willie.

Many flats sharks feed on benthic creatures; and when they're rooting, the disturbed mud and marl cloud the water. Since this is sight-fishing, keep a keen eye out for these "clouds" and for flopping shark tails above the water's surface. Likewise, feeding mullet produce muds, and sharks are often close by, waiting to snap at stragglers. All flats sharks will take a well-placed bait, and a live grass shrimp tops the list. Other good naturals include previously live shrimp, whole finger mullet, and cut ballyhoo. Presentation is perhaps more important than bait, so be cool and cast straight.

Luring Shallow-Water Sharks

Some shark species will take an artificial lure, especially on the flats of southern Florida and in the Caribbean. Blacktips and spinners seem to be the most cooperative, when they're in the mood. Lemon sharks will hit a plug a little more reluctantly but are worth the attempt when they're actively feeding. All sharks hooked on the flats exhibit amazing bursts of speed, not only upon the take but just after hookup. Be ready for this lightning-fast run and have your drag set to allow the fish to rip line from the reel.

Choose a crankbait that makes the least amount of commotion as it hits the water because sharks can be spooky in the shallows. Most effective subsurface artificials mimic a crippled minnow, and they float at rest. Traditional lures include the old Heddon Vamp and a Bass-Oreno rerigged with saltwater hooks. Modern versions are made by Rapala, Pradco, and MirrOlure. The Bomber Jointed Long A, Cordell Jointed Redfin, and original Rebel Jointed Minnow will usually elicit a response.

In the shallows, sharks readily smack a floating plug twitched under the surface on the retrieve. A skinny jointed Rapala works exceedingly well, especially if its lip is

trimmed with a pair of pliers to keep it from diving too deep. The lure should dart a few inches under water during a side-to-side retrieve, teasingly ahead of the following shark. A spinner or lemon can accelerate in the twinkle of an eye, taking the plug in an instant and throwing spray when it does.

Recently we ran into a pod of lemon sharks while casting at the shallow inlet at Tortuguero, Costa Rica. The fish were following the crankbait to the skiff without touching it, so we impaled a piece of freeze-dried squid onto the rear treble and made another cast. It landed directly in front of a

Threadlining Meccas

Sharks always prove that they are indeed "game" fish when taken on a light wand. During the past decade, the multitude of "Vacant" spots in the IGFA's light-line categories have all but disappeared as anglers discover that light tackle has its special rewards. Some shark species behave better with light drag, which is the hallmark of the sport. Welterweight requiems roll up less frequently on light gear, so blue whalers and tope make appropriate opponents. And small mackerel sharks are coming to the fore.

No matter where you live, there's a perfect shark for threadlining, although some areas, of course, are better than others. The Florida Keys leads in the numbers game, followed by New South Wales, Australia. We offer this list of the 10 best areas for the 10 most popular sharks, compiled from records of worldwide IGFA catches on 2- to 20-lb-test line:

Species	Location
Blacktip	Florida Keys, U.S.A.
Blue Shark	Port Hacking, New South Wales, Australia
Hammerhead	East Coast of Florida, U.S.A.
Lemon Shark	Costa Rica, Caribbean side
Mako Shark	Port Hacking–Port Stephens, Australia
Porbeagle	Padstow, Cornwall, England
Thresher	Santa Monica Bay, California, U.S.A.
Tiger Shark	Key West, Florida, U.S.A.
Tope	Parengarenga Harbor, New Zealand
White Shark	New South Wales, Australia

5-footer that immediately grabbed the offering. Remember that sharks rely heavily on their sense of smell; if they won't hit an artificial, try a "teaser" or turn to natural baits. Little bonnetheads, no more than 3 feet long, are found on the flats year-round and can be taken with ultralight spinning gear. Because they have small mouths, they won't hit a plug, but they'll grab a well-placed shrimp or a chunk of ballyhoo. All sharks give top performance in the shallows—a visual display for light-tackle enjoyment.

Mark Feldman

Elizabeth Feldman took this former IGFA line-class-record tope in New Zealand—a fine catch on 4-lb test and an ultralight spinning outfit.

8 SHARKS

When tying shark flies, use a set of super jaws, which accommodates big hooks. The Bill Catherwood–style fly is a good flats choice; and the three deep-water versions imitate mackerel, herring, and ballyhoo head chunks.

ON A
FLY

The art of fly-fishing for sharks in the shallows is surprisingly old, going back at least three or four decades. In the days of bamboo, the pioneering team of Frankie and Jimmy Albright took some of fly-rodding's first sharks on the flats off Islamorada. More recently veteran anglers Lefty Kreh, Mark Sosin, and Flip Pallot have caught and released a wide variety of the toothy tribe.

Offshore fly-rodding is a much newer game, perhaps due to the traditional notion that the long rod could not control these creatures in the deep. In the mid-1970s, deep-water California fly-rodders Bob Edgley and Larry Summers pioneered techniques for teasing blue sharks to a fly. They drifted, established a chum slick, and waited for eager customers to show up for dinner, presenting the fly as a piece of chum. It worked great.

After those successes, Steve Sloan hit pay dirt off Long Island during the summer of 1979. The next year, Rip Cunningham took another fly-caught blue on Barry Gibson's *Shark II* in the Gulf of Maine. We tried the long wand that same year and caught a dogfish on a fly (a mortifying fact

revealed here for the first time). The next season, aboard Tom McFall's *Galadriel*, we fared better and took two blue sharks on successive days. Our first fish, an 87-pounder, became known as the "Three-Minute Shark." We went out the next day feeling pretty cocky, but the second shark, a much larger one, took an hour and a half to subdue. So much for easy catches.

A Sharker's Fly Outfit

Sharking fly tackle has to be rugged. An **8- or 9-weight fly rod** may be adequate for a small shark you might spot while bone-fishing on the flats. In the deep, where the quarry may run upwards of 100 pounds, a **10- to 13-weight rod** will usually do the trick. These sizes are excellent as medium-to-heavy sharking tools, and the 10-weight outfit is great for general flats casting.

With few exceptions, these rods are 9 feet long and have tremendous backbone in the lower third of the blank. Often, the largest fly rods have a second cork grip a

A record-size fly-rod blue shark comes to Tom McFall's Galadriel *in the Gulf of Maine.*

graphite, the rod needs a good deal of lifting power. We once checked a number of rods for this quality and discovered that our 10-weight fly rod could lift only 4½ pounds off the floor. Our 12-weight rod could manage 7½ pounds. Today, some makers claim their rods can lift 15 pounds or more; with sharks, more is better.

Fly reels for sharks must have **a high line and backing capacity** and an ultra-smooth drag. Prices run the gamut from affordable to wicked expensive. Many of the modestly priced reels, such as Scientific Angler's System Two models and the Lamson reels, work fine for most sharks. The minimum-size reel should spool 300 yards of 20-lb-test backing—Scientific Angler's 1011, for example. For heavier work a better choice is the System Two 1213, with a capacity of 350 yards of 30-lb backing if used with an abbreviated fly line. In the high-priced spread, we have Fin-Nors, Pates, and SeaMasters. Other serious models, perhaps a bit more pragmatic, include the new Penn International #4 and the Orvis Odyssey.

The choice of fly lines is easy. A **slow-sinking, weight-forward line,** such as the MonoCore (the "slime line") or the Glass Intermediate, works well for short casts into a chum slick. Sharks are subsurface feeders, and floating lines in deep water can keep the fly from getting down to the feeding zone. The disadvantage of a sinking line comes when we have to make another cast: it must be stripped back before it can be lifted from the water. It's not a perfect world, as fly-fishing illustrates. On the flats we use a **floating weight-forward line,** which can be lifted from the water much more easily.

Most fly lines are close to 100 feet long, which is fine on the flats. But in deep

few inches above the casting grip to allow anglers more leverage on a large fish. Please note, however, that a rod taxed to its limit usually breaks just above the second grip, especially if it has a graphite blank.

With this in mind, a few makers have added a bit of E-glass to help eliminate breakage. Joe Fisher, an experienced big-game fly-rodder and blank-maker, has some rugged models in E-glass; and Jack Erskine produces his Bluewater series in a composite of graphite and E-glass. These are top-drawer rods.

Whether anglers go with E-glass or

Mark Sosin

..n admires a fly-caught lemon shark taken on an E-glass rod and a
..ake" Fin-Nor reel. E-glass remains the strongest and most forgiving
..d material, but the early Fin-Nor is now a collector's item.

..use either a **shooting**
..g) or trim a standard
..50 feet. The resistance
..e ripped through the
..ark is often more than
..an withstand. And the
..popping the backing,
..$50 fly line.
..e a minimum of 300
..**king,** 20-lb test for a
..16-lb (or less) tippet.
..ight rod, move up to
..0-lb tippet—as much
..cram onto the spool.
..the fly line with a nail
..bond or with a loop-
to-loop system. The loop-to-loop connec-

tion is stronger, but both work well and
allow the junction to pass freely through the
rod's guides while you're playing a fish. We
make a loop in the backing by using a
Pliobond-coated Bimini twist; and, a loop in
the fly line by whipping it with dental floss,
then coating it with Pliobond.

Shark Flies

Many decades ago sharkologists discovered
that their favorite fish had a favorite color:
bright orange, as in life vests. That's a fairly
gory scenario when we think about it, but it
gives us an insight into fly colors. Fluores-
cent red, yum-yum yellow, and hot pink
should catch the eye of a fish that normally

feeds with its sniffer; so any shark fly should incorporate some bright, reddish color. (Many avid sharkers believe that sharks perceive these colors as blood.)

Offshore, a fly should look like a piece of chum, because the fish will be imprinted on these tidbits by the time it reaches the boat. On the flats a fly can imitate baitfish or shrimp. You've got only a few options with hook size. Big sharks can bite through the wire of hooks smaller than a 4/0 O'Shaughnessy; it's happened to us. But a hook larger than a 6/0 is incredibly difficult to set in a shark's jaw.

When you're tying shark patterns, don't bother to spend the extra time glassing the thread with successive coats of head cement. A shark fly is a one-time affair. Traditional tarpon flies—such as the Bonbright, Strawberry Blond, Apte's Tarpon Fly, and Lefty's Deceiver—will work in deep water. Any large pattern that sinks slowly and has red in it will catch a shark's attention under the right offshore conditions. Sharkers can also design their own patterns. We tie flies with large teddy-bear eyes to represent the chunked head of the "bait of the day." There's nothing like catching a fish on a fly you've tied—even invented—yourself.

Flies tossed on the flats and along shallow bars can imitate baitfish and benthic creatures. Most bonefish-permit flies will interest smaller sharks, and many patterns can be tied on bigger hooks. The Brown Snapping Shrimp, Catherwood's Crab, Antron Crabs, Clouser Deep Minnows, and Pink Crazy Charlies are just a few patterns that can interest smaller sharks like bonnetheads.

Larger flats species, such as blacktips and lemons, will take baitfish patterns like the Catherwood series tied by Umpqua Fly Tiers. The original deer-hair floaters designed by Bill Catherwood, the grand old master of saltwater flies, are very good patterns (see photo on page 96). Floating flies that "slurp" under the surface on the retrieve, such as Catherwood's and Larry Dahlberg's divers, are perhaps the most effective. A complete list of flies would be endless; and with sharks, presentation is perhaps more important than pattern.

Rigging Fly Leaders

The big-game fly leaders available through some fly-fishing outfitters are all tied with a heavy mono shock leader ahead of the tippet. That won't help with sharks unless we attach our own length of wire to the mono shocker. But with a few spare hours, we can make our own leaders.

First, attach a short leader butt (no longer than 3 feet), made from 40- or 50-lb-test mono, to the end of the fly line with a nail knot or an Albright knot. We prefer the Albright because it's strong. At the other end of the butt, make a 2-inch loop with a double surgeon's knot.

Next, build a tippet. Starting with 8 feet of 16- or 20-lb-test mono, double a little less than 2 feet of line at each end with a Bimini knot, making a tippet about 2 feet long between the doubled ends. We tie the Bimini using our right knee to hold the loop. With a little practice, this knee method will make a clean single-person Bimini; the rollover step can be aided by a pull at the "double" with a finger. Double one end again, using a double surgeon knot and making it large enough that a fly will fit through the loop. Keep the other doubled end as short as possible when you attach it to the wire shocker with an Albright knot. Heavy wire,

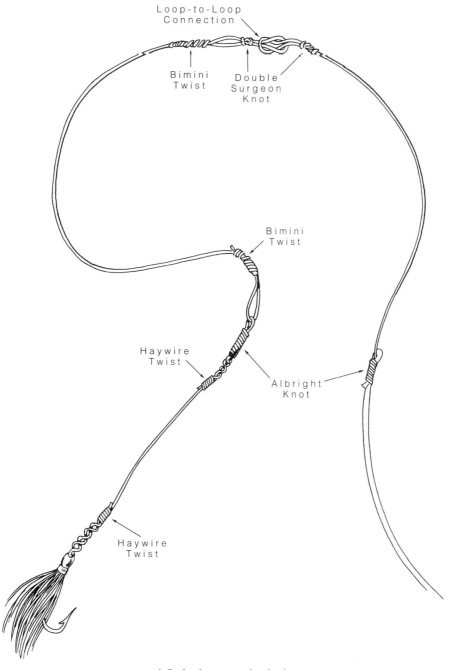

Loop-to-Loop
Connection

Bimini
Twist

Double
Surgeon
Knot

Bimini
Twist

Haywire
Twist

Albright
Knot

Haywire
Twist

A fly-leader system for sharks.

which won't cut through the mono under heavy pressure, makes the best shock leader.

Use a simple, loop-to-loop connection to tie the finished tippet section and attached fly to the butt section. This quick and easy method allows you to change flies quickly. We recommend that you have an assortment of backup flies on hand, tippets attached, in the event of a break-off.

If by chance you're after a fly-rod world record, remember that the tippet must conform to IGFA standards. The total length of a wire shocker, from the tippet end of the Bimini knot to the hook-eye, must be no more than 12 inches—mighty short abrasion insurance. At the same time, the single strand of tippet material must be at least 15 inches long. Sanctioned fly-rodding for sharks is tough, especially offshore. The cast (unlike in billfishing) is made from a dead boat, with the engines shut down; the advantage of instant maneuverability is lost.

We suggest that beginning fly-rodders catch a few sharks with a somewhat longer, nonsanctioned shock tippet for starters. They'll land more fish and have more fun. There's plenty of time for records down the road. We use the IGFA tippet dimensions, and quite frankly, we lose a lot of sharks. A few years ago, in a fit of poor judgment, we hooked and fought an estimated 250-pound blue shark by sanctioned standards. It was the biggest fish we ever lost on a fly.

Offshore Fly-Rodding for Sharks

There is nothing to match the thrill of catching a large blue-water animal on a fly rod. Most opportunities occur during a flat-calm day of chumming for blue sharks and makos. That's when ideal fish are sighted at boatside. It really helps to wear a pair of sunglasses with gray polarized lenses whenever you fish in deep zones whether the water is blue or green. Usually anglers will use conventional gear but with a fly outfit rigged and standing by in a forward corner of the cockpit, out of harm's way and waiting for a nice little shark of less than 100 pounds to come sniffing around the chum basket. When we spot that shark, we cut a couple of bait chunks and toss them at the fish. If it takes a chunk, we see the whites of its eyes for a split second because, whenever a shark takes a bite, the nictitating membrane rolls up and covers the eye for protection against a scratched retina. Ain't that odd!

This biological adaptation is a great aid to the fly-rodder. The shark will circle, looking for more chunks, and we try to drop the fly just off to one side of its oncoming path. We watch the fly sink slowly, and watch the shark. There! The fly is gone in a blink of the shark's white eyelid. Wait until the fish's eye turns dark again and set the hook solidly with a side-sweep or direct pull on the line—before the fish can swallow the fly. Ideally, we want the fly to set in the corner of the jaw, just inside the teeth, so that the maximum amount of wire leader will remain outside the shark's mouth. We'll need all the wire we can get.

If by some chance the shark passes by the fly but doesn't take it, leave the fly in the water. Quite often, a fish will make one more complete circle and nail the offering. Once the shark is hooked, be careful not to step on the exiting fly line as we often do. (Floppy shoelaces on deck shoes also snag a fly line, so tie your laces with a square knot and trim the excess.) To guide the exiting fly line without creating a snarl, make a circle with your left thumb and forefinger,

*A fly that is perfectly set in a shark's jaw allows a maximum
of wire leader material to remain outside the mouth.*

keeping your arm well away from the rod butt and reel. Once the line is on the reel, you can breathe a temporary sigh of relief.

While all these shenanigans are going on, someone has to cast off the chum ball, and the boat handler starts the engine (or engines). As we've said before, the boat must position the shark off either stern quarter and actually lead the fish. Sometimes a shark will race aft, and the boat will have to back down. We're trying to avoid the angle at which the shark's sandpaper body will rub against the tippet. If that happens, the fight's over.

In the worst of cases, and it happens often enough, the shark will sound and head for the depths. Then angler and skipper must ascertain the fish's direction and lead it just slightly. A sounding fish is actually pulling the entire fly line and backing through the water vertically, creating a bow that will often pop the tippet section.

Weeds and flotsam can also stress a tippet to its breaking point. If a fly line runs into a kelp paddy or across a line of floating rockweed, the stuff hangs on, slowly adding weight and resistance. Maneuver the rod tip and boat to stay clear of these hang-ups. With all the potential for mishap, taking a blue-water shark on fly tackle is a major accomplishment.

As this relatively new sport develops,

we believe some truly large fish will be taken. The current deep-water shark record stands at 184 pounds, so it's possible that a sharker will top the magic 200 mark before the tarpon fly-rodders do. For record blue sharks, the best time and place may be August in the Gulf of Maine. And for makos, usually smaller fly-rod fish, the prime locations include New Zealand from January through March, and California in the summer.

Small great whites, porbeagles, and threshers are seldom caught on light tackle, even by baiting; and none have yet been taken on a fly. We suspect that these deeper-water sharks have never shown at boatside under the right circumstances but that they will one day follow the blues and makos that have been successfully fly-fished in deeper zones. Meanwhile, a host of mid-depth requiems awaits the feather merchants.

A 62-pound tiger shark recently showed at Captain Ken Harris's *Finesse* out of Key West and was fly-caught by Rick Gunion. He now holds the first fly-rod world record for that species. Hammerheads are among the few other shallow-water sharks that have been taken on the long wand. The largest, weighing 106½ pounds, was also fly-caught near Key West by Mike Stidham. And South Florida's flats, of course, host the famous spinners and lemon sharks, the most common species taken in skinny water.

Fly-Rodding the Flats

Many of the methods discussed in "Spinning and Casting on the Flats" (Chapter 7) also apply to fly-rodders. While dumping a bait and sinker near a shark in the shallows may cause it to steam off for distant quarters, a properly placed fly can be less spooky. So, in some ways, a fly rod can actually be an advantage. On the other hand, we have to be able to make an accurate and sometimes long cast. Distance is not our personal strong point; a long cast for us is about 60 feet, with the wind at our back. But a 60-foot cast is often all that's needed.

Fly-anglers can use a **floating line** in the shallows and a longer leader. And they can use smaller fly patterns since flats sharks tend to be lighter than their blue-water cousins. We also recommend floating flies because, if we make a poorly aimed cast with a floating setup, we can rip the line off the surface and reposition the fly in one, quick, false cast. This is faster and easier than stripping a sinking line back to within 20 feet of the skiff before making a corrected cast. We should point out, however, that tearing the line from the surface is a great way to spook a nearby fish.

Sharking on the flats is a stalking game, almost like hunting. We are stalking the shark; and the shark is stalking shrimp, minnows, crabs, small rays, and almost anything that moves or burrows under the marl. Its fare is entirely different from the bits of chum that entice deep-water sharks. So our flies must look like a shallow-water meal.

The techniques used in fly-fishing the flats are just about the same as in spin-fishing and bait-casting. Be there for the incoming tide, keep your peepers peeled for slow-moving and finning sharks, and pole the skiff to a spot where a cast will drop just ahead of but not too close to the fish. Some casters make a slightly long cast, working the fly across the shark's path as it approaches.

Do not position a fly so that it must be retrieved toward the fish as it's stripped back. Baitfish are supposed to flee from

A New England blue shark taken on a 16-lb tippet. The fish weighed 127 pounds and was caught on an Otto Zwarg reel and boron 10-weight rod.

*Flats situations are always exciting, especially with fly-rod sharks,
and care is needed at boatside.*

sharks, not attack them. After the cast, try to get the shark's attention by stripping the fly with a little surface commotion. An interested fish will often come up behind the fly, even snaking off to one side and then the other as it tries to figure out what "this thing" is. Then, kaboom, its snout tosses water as it grabs the fly.

Make sure the fish has the fly in its jaws, then set the hook in a **sideways thrust**, and clear the line while the fish screams off for "some place else," as King Friday would say. Once the fish settles down, the poler can keep it to one side of the angler. If the fish is bigger than expected and digs in for a tow, a fly-rodder can exert **side pressure**: alternating sides, maintain steady pressure on one side of the fish for four or five minutes before swinging the rod to the other side with enough force to unbalance the fish (even if it means dipping your rod under water). Pressure like this can wear down a fish faster than an upward pull.

Many anglers don't use a boat on the flats; wading slowly through knee-deep waters, they take a lot of sharks. Wear tough-soled shoes when you're wading, and slide your feet along the bottom instead of taking actual steps as you would on dry land. Your feet will then just tap against any stingray hidden in the sand or mud, and it can zip off to safer quarters. If, however, you step on a ray, it will swipe you with its well-armed tail. Better to disturb the sand and cloud the water than to make a trip to a distant emergency room.

All flats fish are tough to see, so wear a pair of quality sunglasses with brown or amber polarized lenses. A wide-brimmed, straw "Charlie Waterman Hat" will also come in handy for shading your eyes, ears, and neck. A double-brimmed "Mark Sosin Hat" is also a good choice. Whenever you're fishing the flats or any tropical locale, use a generous amount of sunblock, SPF-15 or higher.

Fish while the tide is up—quality angling time ebbs with it. And after a few hours, the sharks will snake their way back to deeper waters to cruise outside until the next coming tide.

9

DOWN

The rabid shark from hell! Good boat maneuvering and good wiring practices can prevent losing situations like this one.

TO THE WIRE

It's a great day on the shark grounds when a submerged mountain peak or productive drop-off yields a great fish. Depending on the area fished and the tackle used, the great fish could be a 50-pound tope taken on 8-lb-test line or a 100-pound blue shark caught on a fly. A big mackerel shark or hammerhead would make the day for those who fish the heavy threads. But if they are not the stuff of records, all these great fish are released. We have returned some wonderful fish to the sea. Some were "premature releases," but that's part of the sharking experience.

A combination of good boat handling and angler awareness leads to the successful capture and release of the great fish. Getting "down to the wire" is a reward for correct decisions; the actual wiring and tagging or the gaffing are another kettle of fish entirely. First, however, we must get the shark to the boat. It's hooked, and it's getting tired; things are looking good. Throughout the battle, the boat's complement has worked as a sharking team. Each person on board fills the billet as the angler, the boat handler, the wire man, and

the gaffer (or release team's tagger). Fish as a team.

Boat Positioning

The fish has given us several runs and remains in sight as it gets close to the boat. Our angler sees the knot of the double line emerging from the water, and the boat handler or skipper positions the fish at the cockpit quarter. With a twin-engine boat, keeping just one engine in gear is sometimes all that's required for this maneuver. Aboard single-engine craft, the boat handler keeps the engine near idle and takes a small amount of rudder. While the boat makes a slow, wide circle, the angler pumps the double line onto the reel. The shark is led to the boat smooth and easy; we don't want to spook him.

Throughout these last minutes, the skipper has his hands on the gears and throttles. At the ready, he can slip the other engine into gear and use both throttles if the fish decides to make a last-ditch effort. When possible, the boat handler will try to lead big fish to the windward side of the cockpit. And the wire man stands next to the angler at this time. (In parts of the globe, this "wire man"—of either gender—is also called a cockpit man, and in Australia, a deckie.) The shark is now within 20 feet of the side of the boat.

Wiring Techniques

The wire man must wear a pair of **cut-resistant gloves** to protect his or her hands from the leader, which can cut right to the bone with the weight of the fish. Some fishing gloves are made from a plastic-reinforced mesh; others are sewn from heavy leather and look like the old-fashioned welder's gloves. Either style works well, but for really large fish, we recommend that a pair of cotton gloves be worn under leather ones for added protection against the intense pressure a big shark can exert—it can cut off your circulation. *Never, under any circumstance, grab a wire leader without gloves when a fish is thrashing at the other end.*

The wire man should **at all times wear fishing pliers** in a case on the trouser belt. When the shark is held boatside, it's not a good time for the wire man to be back at a tackle station groping for fishing pliers (see photo on page 108).

When you've got a large shark in deep water, grasp the conventional leader when the angler's line swivel comes within a foot of the rod tip. Some deckies like to use the swivel as the initial handhold, but a Coast-lock snap can be opened by the wire man's grab. A McMahon snap-swivel, though, can be grasped without dire consequences. For many medium-size sharks, like blues and duskies, the wire is hauled in by successive grabs without taking any wraps. For large fish, take a wrist-rolling **double wrap** on the wire before it slips due to the shark's weight, and use alternating handgrabs to take additional wraps to smoothly haul the fish alongside the cockpit. When the wire is grabbed, the stand-up angler steps back from the rail, lessening the drag a bit just in case the fish bolts from the wire man's grasp.

Sharks fought from a chair are a bit easier to wire. Throughout the fight, a team member has swiveled the chair to keep the angler's rod pointing at the shark. If a big fish runs to one side and the chair does not swing with it, the result is often a broken chair gimbal. When the angler gets those last few feet of double line in, the wire man has room to step in front of the seated angler and grab the leader. Here, too, the angler slips the reel's drag to a lesser tension (not *free-spool*) and waits at the alert, just in case "someone" gets overpowered.

The initial wiring of any shark will be the easiest one. If the fish makes a dangerous spurt for freedom, unroll the grasp and let the leader go. There is no shame in allowing the fish to take another run; and in most cases, the shark will strip just a few feet of double line from the angler's reel. When the shark is pumped back, retake the wraps, but remember that the fish is now wary and will struggle harder to stay away from the boat.

Throughout the wiring and impending release, the boat keeps a small amount of forward momentum. With the engine(s) in gear, a shark can continue swimming—something it cannot do beside a dead boat—thus avoiding a leader-tangling roll as the excited fish wraps itself around the wire.

With a shark swimming at boatside, an experienced wire man can slide an opened pair of pliers down the leader, getting as close as possible to the jaws before

Mesh gloves, usually interwoven with Kevlar or other strong plastics, are fine for wiring smaller sharks.

a dangerous snip be attempted.

Small flats sharks that have been taken by light-tackle plugging or on a fly can be wired with a traditional **salmon tailer**. This old device, invented in 19th-century England and still sold by Hardy Brothers, has been modified for saltwater use. Mark Sosin was instrumental in the transition, and the modern, longer-handle flats version is now a stock item at Aftco. The use of a tailer is the best and most humane way to capture a shark until the angler can pop the artificial plug from the jaw area. Seldom is a plug swallowed; the fish usually carries it in the corner of its mouth. With the plug removed, the tailer's wire loop is slackened, and the released shark can swim off unhurt and may even continue feeding.

We strongly urge that you give a great deal of care to any shark about to be released. Lifting the animal high out of the water can cause internal injuries—broken membranes for the shark and a hernia or wrenched back for the wire man. So, at least from the gill slits aft, keep the body of the fish in the water while lures are removed or pictures taken.

Tagging Sharks for Science

A shark can be tagged before it's released to provide scientific data should it ever be recaptured. Tagged sharks have lived at large for decades, crossing oceans and logging thousands upon thousands of miles, often to be caught again by another angler in a distant country. One shark was at large for 27 years before recapture. The tags, tagging cards, and applicator darts are available from the National Marine Fisheries Service laboratory in Narragansett, Rhode

snipping the wire. Just how close a person's hand should get to the animal's teeth usually depends on the species and the deckie's ability. Smaller sharks can curl their body out of the water and go for a hand, but larger sharks have more difficulty arching. Many shark fishers have been grazed or bitten at this point, so please take extreme care during the release procedure. An experienced person can often clip the wire at the location of the haywire twist and the hook-eye. We believe that a hook will leave a released shark quicker if the entire leader has been cut away. Only after releasing many sharks of different sizes, should such

Island, run by Dr. Jack Casey (see Appendix 3 for the address).

Remember that 54 percent of all sharks tagged in the NMFS program are tagged by sporting anglers. Many states, including California, have tagging programs, and internationally so do Great Britain and Australia.

Shark **tagging sticks**, with the applicator, are sold by local tackle dealers, and anglers can make their own. We keep two sticks on board the *Lucky Star II;* one is a homemade jobbie that looks and works great. We used an old fiberglass blank from a very used 30-lb-class trolling rod, and removed the guides with a knife and acetone.

Other sharkers can do the same and save a good deal of money: With a propane torch, apply heat to the male ferrule below the grip to remove it; replace the ferrule

with a rubber crutch cap. Trim the top of the blank until the NMFS applicator slips loosely into it; then epoxy it in place and overwrap it with rod thread. Glue a cylindrical EVA foam stopper over the end of the blank containing the butt of the applicator; this allows the dart to enter the fish's flesh to a depth of 1¼ inches.

Slip the tag over the groove in the applicator tip and hold it in place with a couple of wraps of a rubber band. The tagger should take careful aim for the area at the rear base of the first dorsal fin. In this part of the shark's body, the flesh and muscle are thick, and there are no major arteries that could be severed by mistake.

We have discovered that thrashing and rolling sharks are the worst to tag, so we keep the boat in gear and the fish swimming. The slow-moving fish, directly off to

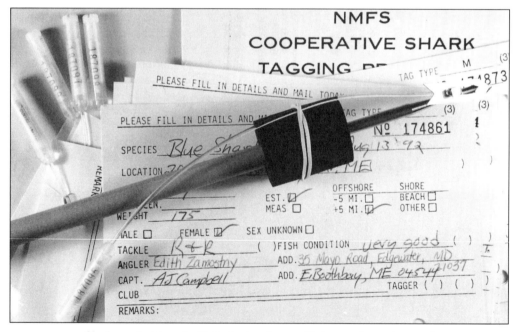

Sharks are best tagged with the boat underway. Make sure the tag is secured
with a rubber band that will break after placement.

the side of the cockpit, is an easy target for proper tag placement. If the shark is large and thrashing the b'jabbers out of the side of the boat, release the fish immediately to keep it from hurting itself any further. Forget about tagging it. There will be plenty of sharks to tag, and letting a few go without fanfare can sometimes be the humane course to take.

Once a shark is tagged, its size, weight, and either its total or fork length must be accurately determined so that you can properly fill out the postage-paid, returnable tagging cards before you mail them back to the Cooperative Shark Tagging Program. The fish's sex must be ascertained as well. Males have ventral fins modified into long sausage-shaped claspers, and of course females don't. If the fish has prenuptial "bite marks," don't check the ventrals, because only females carry these scars. As a rule of thumb for length-to-weight comparison, blue sharks and tope weigh less than many members of the clan, makos seem to weigh more, and porbeagles are downright overweight. If the data on the original tagging card is accurate, everybody gains solid information.

Gaffing Equipment

In any season some sharks are taken as state, province, or world records, but more are kept to be eaten. Edible sharks, in order

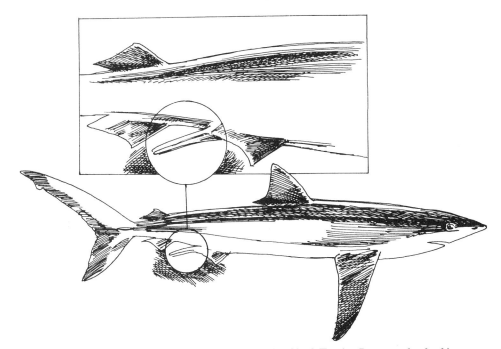

When you return tagging cards to the Cooperative Shark Tagging Program, the shark's sex must be listed. Male sharks have ventral fins modified into long sausage-shaped claspers.

of superb to poor taste, include makos, porbeagles, threshers, hammerheads, tope, duskies, leopards, doggies, and blue sharks. We have tried eating blue sharks on a number of occasions and still find the flesh unpalatable. But we've talked to party-boat clients who claim they enjoy blue-shark steaks. Whether for records or meals, sharks should be handled properly at boatside, and dangerous situations must be avoided.

Sharkers have a wide variety of **fixed gaffs, flying gaffs, cockpit harpoons,** and **tail ropes** to choose from. A number of manufacturers—Reliable, Canyon Products, and Aftco among them—produce rugged, quality gaffs with hefty aluminum shafts. The hook and handle for a flying gaff

are usually sold separately. For managing heavy mackerel sharks, a **meat hook** comes in handy. It's nothing more than a giant gaff hook with a handgrip at one end.

Fixed gaffs need a handle at least 1 inch in diameter and 5 to 6 feet long. We like a small gaff hook with a 3½-inch throat and a heavier-wired, medium gaff with a 4-inch gap. Some of the newer fixed gaffs have hooks up to 7 inches. Much like flying gaffs, the fixed models feature a fiberglass handle and an eye at the hook for attaching a line. The large fixed gaff can really control heavy sharks.

Flying gaffs with a gap of 5 inches or more are made with a double-grip, removable, 6-foot handle and a rope attached to

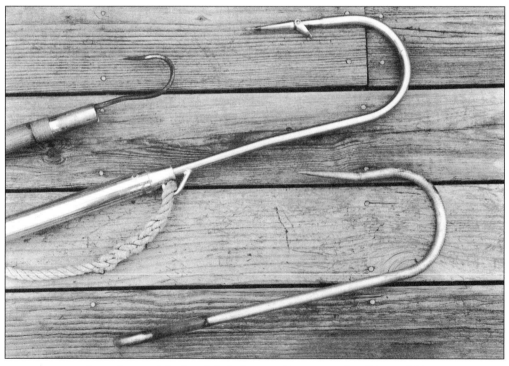

A complement of shark tools includes a small tungsten tail gaff (upper left),
a standard flying gaff (middle), and a meat hook.

the hook that allows the hook to slip off the handle once the fish is gaffed. Rig a flying gaff so that the line can reach either cockpit quarter, allowing freedom of movement at the business end in the water. We attach the end of the gaff line with a double clove hitch to the fighting-chair stanchion where it meets the deck. This is a good central tie-down, but other anglers in the cockpit must remain clear of the line during the gaffing.

A flying-gaff hook is held in place by a notch, and in the Reliable model, a twist of the handle releases it. Some hooks are held by tension from the attached line, which usually follows the handle up to a notch on the top and then comes back down to the upper grip area, where it is held in place. Additional tension can be applied by a single wrap of electrical tape around the handle and line. Once the hook is buried in the fish, the tape must break to allow the gaff to immediately slip from the handle. Otherwise, a large twisting fish can bend the gaff's aluminum handle. With this breakaway setup, the removed handle is stowed, and the shark is tethered to the gaff line. Flying gaffs can be dangerous when used on outsized mackerel sharks, because the fish can go flying and the gaff hook can too, sometimes flying back at the boat's occupants. That's why they're called flying gaffs.

A cockpit harpoon solves this problem and is a good alternative to the flying gaff. Although it's not allowed for IGFA records, it is nonetheless the safest device for "gaffing" large makos. The harpoon handle is 6 to 8 feet long; a **detachable dart** is fitted to a Morse taper at the tip of the harpoon shank. A short length of multi-strand wire, attached to a longer nylon line, is crimped to the dart head, much as tuna fishermen do it. The cockpit harpoon is not for a "green"

fish—the shark should be tired and ready for the coup de grace. With the harpoon line attached to a cleat, the worst that can happen is a pulled dart. The cockpit harpoon is one of the best and most underrated landing tools at a sharker's disposal.

The Art of Gaffing and Tailing

Sharks are the most difficult fish to gaff. They twist and snake in ways that only a contortionist could admire; makos even try to jump at boatside—not a very nice fish at all. Smaller sharks, generally under 100 pounds, can be taken with a medium-size 4-inch straight gaff. It is very important to immobilize the shark by getting its propeller out of the water. So aim for the area in back of the major dorsal fin. If a shark such as a mako is gaffed too far forward, it can use its tail to make a leap—a dangerous situation. You could end up with a live mackerel shark in the cockpit.

If the shark exceeds 100 pounds, a large fixed or flying gaff is the appropriate tool since big sharks can straighten smaller gaff hooks, bend aluminum handles, or (heaven forbid) snap the wooden handle of that classic gaff you've just built. With the 7-inch gaff hook in place, tightly wrap the gaff rope to a cockpit cleat.

With active sharks over 200 pounds, consider the cockpit harpoon before using the 7-inch gaff and tail gaff. To control the shark's flailing tail—always dangerous but especially so with threshers—a medium or smaller fixed gaff can be pulled into the fish just above the swell where the body tapers to the fish's keel area. This will help stabilize the shark for the tail-roper.

Making a Custom Gaff

Production gaffs and meat grabbers are designed with a stainless steel hook. It never rusts, but in the smaller wire, it can straighten under the pressure of a big fish. Mustad still makes a selection of **tempered steel gaff hooks;** anglers have to attach their own handles. Quite frankly, we have always liked the bend and strength of the Mustad tungsten gaff hooks even though they rust, so we take the time to fashion our own custom jobbies.

A homemade fixed gaff can look sharp, and it won't bend like the aluminum types. We go to a hardware store for replacement garden-rake handles of prefinished hickory. A hickory rake handle has the strength you need; and affixed to a standard gaff hook, it will usually float vertically if you accidentally drop it overboard.

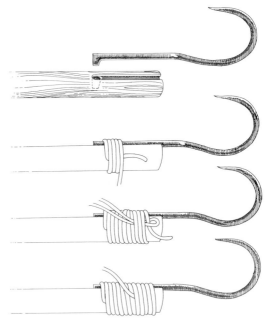

To make a traditional wooden gaff, purchase a gaff hook with a 3- to 4-inch throat, and pick a good straight-grain handle. Mustad gaff hooks come with a pin or tang, bent at 90 degrees, which goes into a hole you drill into the handle, about 4 or 5 inches from the end. For a tight fit, drill this hole a little smaller than the tang but not so small that the wood will split when the tang is tapped in.

Cut a shallow groove with a table saw, from the tang hole to the handle end, to accept the shank of the gaff hook. Make the groove deep enough to take the shank width of a 3- or 3½-inch hook, and about half the shank width of a 4-inch gaff hook. This leaves maximum strength in the handle for the larger hook's wire size. Then, lay the hook shank over the groove and hole, and tap it in place.

Wrap the entire length of the hook-shank area with twisted nylon heading twine. Start by tightly wrapping the twine over its initial end, continue the wrap down to about ½ inch from the lower end, slip a separate loop of twine under the wrap, and continue to the extreme end of the shaft. Cut the wrap, leaving about ½ inch of twine at this tag end, and carefully pull it under the wrap by tugging on the loop until the end disappears. Finish the wrap with several coats of varnish.

We add two more wraps to the wooden handle as upper and lower grips at the points where the handle is grasped during gaffing. This adds a touch of class and makes for a better grip. Alternatively, you can drill a hole in the end of a used male trolling-rod ferrule, fitting it over the hook shank and the end of the handle and epoxying it in place before making the finishing wrap. The resulting gaff is strong and graceful. With maintenance and revarnishing through the years, it can become a cherished possession.

Dave Elm

Captains Sue Curwen and Barry Smith gaff a blue shark on the party boat Yellow Bird. *Headboat gaffs must be long, with handles made from hardwood or Tonkin bamboo.*

Use double gaffs on larger sharks, such as this thresher. A third gaff can be used to control the dangerous tail.

Securing a tail rope.

Bang Sticks and Firearms?

In the career of every shark angler there comes the first time an edible or record fish is at boatside. Commercial fishermen kill sharks en masse and think nothing of it. We have discovered that it's not easy to dispatch an occasional animal, but sometimes the job must be done.

In many cases, smaller specimens will expire on their own if they are bled by an incision just below the gill slits. Make the cut until it's obvious that you've located a major artery, and then try to do the same on the other side of the fish. Usually the fish will pump itself dry. If a shark taken for eating is bled while its heart is still beating, its steaks will have a superior taste.

The exact point when a shark expires is not easy to determine; its motor reflexes may continue even after it's dead. As Billy Crystal would say, the shark is "mostly dead but not totally dead!" Therefore, never stick your hand into a shark's mouth. Some say the fish is dead when the eye glasses over and turns concave, but this sounds more like an "extremely dead" fish to us.

Some species with white bellies will blush pink after expiration, as the capillaries break near the skin's surface. Threshers actually bleed through the surface of the tail, as expert California sharker Dave Elm discovered when he ran his hand along the tail of a "totally dead" thresher and found that blood had seeped through the pores. The fact remains that some sharks take forever to die, and anglers often want to hasten the process. Small sharks can be dispatched with a persuader, a small heavy club such as the one made by Aftco. We do not use a "priest," because it seems to offer nothing

Tail ropes come in two styles: some stock models have a length of braided wire spliced into a longer section of line; others are made entirely from line. But all tail ropes should have a loop spliced into the end.

We can't lasso the flopping tails of most large sharks in the popular manner, and our experience tells us that, unless you're Will Rogers, you probably can't either. We recommend a much easier method. Slip the loop end of the tail rope around the small of the body, just forward of the tail, and pass the other end of the rope through the loop, pulling it tight— your shark has been tailed, and you can cleat the animal off. On any prized shark, we pass the tag end of the tail rope around the shark and under itself twice more in a reversed direction. The resulting clove hitch, added to the tailing loop, keeps the rope from working loose, which could allow a dying and very edible fish to accidentally sink into the depths as crab food.

more than unnecessary violence. Hang a small shark off the bow cleat and it will expire—eventually. A larger shark is tougher to handle; but you can usually work on it after it has stopped thrashing.

Never bring a live shark into a boat. Sharks are dangerous enough in the water. You do not ever want to be in a boat with an infuriated shark; it is the worst situation anglers can place themselves in. There is also a remote yet distinct possibility that a large mackerel shark, tiger, or thresher thrashing at boatside could endanger the structural integrity of the craft. For the extreme emergency, keep a 12-gauge bang stick handy but stowed well out of the reach of juniors; it's the safest dispatching weapon available, but it can do massive bodily harm.

We do not go along with the haphazard use of guns on board vessels. Sharkers are supposed to be fishing, not re-enacting the Wild West. Firearms should never be used by a person who has not taken a proper, sanctioned gun-safety course, and most shark anglers have not. Captain Matt Wilder and I are knowledgeable in firearms safety, and we keep a stainless steel .357 magnum revolver in a Secret Place where customers and even close friends cannot find it. It's there just in case it's needed; but in all our years of professional sharking, we have never used the pistol.

Preparing Sharks for the Table

After immediate bleeding, any shark destined for a gourmet meal should be dressed promptly. Makos and porbeagles are the only sharks we know of that can hang overboard for more than an hour. Perhaps it's their warm-blooded makeup, but mackerel sharks do not seem to develop the rancid, uremic flesh that all other species do. Blue sharks are the most uremic and need to be eviscerated and steaked haste-amundo. The smaller sharks are the best for eating because they can be handled more quickly after capture and more efficiently during the cleaning process.

Sharp fillet knives are required for prepping sharks (see illustration, page 120), and we do mean "knives" because the first knife will dull during the ripping and chunking procedure. To dress any shark, cut a rip from the vent forward to the throat, and remove the head and the entrails. Then clean the body cavity with a little salt water and cut the side flaps away. Each side flap will end up looking like a giant tapered fillet, and it can be cut away from the skin to produce several meal-size portions.

To remove the cartilaginous "backbone," lay the fish upside down and, working toward the tail, make intersecting cuts on each side of the backbone, penetrating the flesh just enough to lift the bone out. When you reach the tail area, cut the bone and tail free, and discard.

Next, cut the fish into three or four (depending on its size) large chunks, using the same knife, which will then be as dull as an old spade. Switch to a sharp fillet knife and make a lengthwise cut down through the meat along the center of the shark chunk, where the backbone was, and be sure not to cut through the skin. The flesh will fall into two long loins still attached on the bottom to the skin. With the sharp knife and with the skin side remaining flat on the cutting board, saw along the inside of the skin to remove the meaty chunk.

When the skin has been removed, cut the large chunks of meat into ¾- to 1-inch-thick steaks. Put the steaks and flap fillets

Keep shark-dressing knives sharp by stoning them. We recommend a couple of fillet knives and a larger splitting (butcher) knife for removing the head and tail.

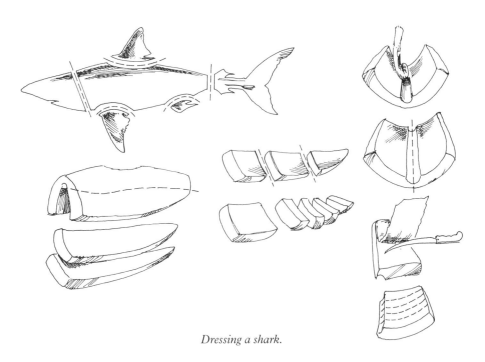

Dressing a shark.

Lemon and Garlic Shark Steaks

What better way to celebrate a great catch than to invite the crew to a barbecued steak dinner. This recipe is a favorite of ours—a real palate-pleaser.

Ingredients:

4 to 6 mako or thresher steaks	½ cup Chardonnay
5 tbsp. olive oil	juice of 2 lemons
3 or 4 garlic cloves, chopped	pinch of cayenne pepper
¼ cup fresh basil, chopped	

Combine the wine, oil, lemon juice, garlic, pepper, and one half of the basil, in a large bowl to make the marinade. Pat the shark steaks dry with a paper towel; place them in the marinade for about an hour, and turn them occasionally for even distribution.

Remove the steaks and place them over a very hot barbecue for about 10 minutes—5 minutes on each side. Empty the marinade into a skillet, and reduce it over heat while the steaks are cooking. Remove the shark steaks from the grill and arrange them on a platter. Add the remaining fresh basil to the reduced marinade and pour the marinade over the fish before serving.

This recipe can be varied; you may, for example, want to substitute fresh oregano or dill for the basil. If you broil the steaks, add 2 minutes to the cooking time (12 minutes total) and turn them after 6 minutes.

into 1-gallon Ziploc bags and immediately store them in a cooler on ice. The quick and proper preparation of a shark ensures that the fish will get rave reviews when it's presented at a special dinner.

We dress sharks at sea so that the head and skin can be dropped overboard in deep water, where they will be eaten by benthic scavengers. Cleaning fish at the dock or marina is a breach of etiquette, often grossing out nearby boaters who eat meat but cannot accept the notion that an animal goes through a gory process before its meat is packed in neat little shrink-wrapped thingies at a supermarket.

Shark steaks and flap fillets can be marinated in the chef's secret flavorings and cooked any number of ways. The flesh is moist and often tastes less gamey than that of other big fish; those who enjoy the taste of swordfish will be happy with mackerel-shark and thresher steaks. And unlike the flesh of many other animals and fish, shark meat is low in oil and cholesterol. It can be frozen for several months without getting freezer burn like some of the oilier fishes such as salmon and tuna. It can be baked, broiled, or barbecued. Shark can be deep-fried too, of course, if one doesn't mind all that breading and grease. We are avid barbecuers, and to us an outdoor-grilled fresh mako steak is next to heaven.

10

SHARKING

Kurt Christensen with a big Gulf of Maine thresher. Although never common enough, a few threshers are taken in these northern New England waters each season.

Kurt Christensen

U.S.A.

Along the East Coast of the United States, anglers will discover some of the globe's finest sharking. Temperate species dominate the regions from northern New England to Chesapeake Bay, and the areas from Virginia to the Gulf of Mexico offer tropical breeds. The West Coast holds both cold- and warm-water species, with light-tackle soupfin and leopard sharks in upper California, and excellent mako and thresher angling in southern waters.

The Great Gulf of Maine

The Gulf of Maine stretches from Nova Scotia's Sable Island to Cape Cod and has more shoreline than the rest of the East Coast combined. The region hosts the highest number of blue sharks in the northern hemisphere, and they are among the largest in the world. In recent years, makos have been discovered, ranging from 35 pounds to well over a grand. The Gulf of Maine also has a small seasonal population of visiting threshers and great whites.

The "great white death," as Zane Grey described it, has never been taken on rod and reel in Gulf of Maine waters as far as we know. Fishing out of Camden, Maine, in 1953, S. B. Parker and his nine-year-old son, George, harpooned a great white near Mark Island. They were in a 19-foot skiff, the shark "leaped entirely clear of the water," and it took them an hour and a half to get a tail rope around the fish. The next season, Parker and son were again fishing in Penobscot Bay when they ironed another white shark. This one was weighed; it tipped the scales at 927 pounds. In 1992 two white sharks were sighted south of the Kettle Ground, 25 miles below Boothbay Harbor, and one of them was munching on a dead whale.

Following Captain Jim Hinkley's capture of a 689-pound mako in 1990, anglers pushed the state record to the present 727-pound mark. Two larger makos, one weighing 915 pounds and one just over a grand, have been harpooned by tuna fishermen. We have personally seen two makos that would easily exceed a half ton. August is the month for makos in the Gulf of Maine.

Blue sharks are plentiful, and on a

good August day as many as a dozen fish can be tagged. In 1990, we released a fat 13-footer that was very close to the all-tackle record, and sharks above 300 pounds are returned to these temperate waters every year. The blue whalers are present from July to September, and sometimes into October during a warm fall.

The top fishing grounds in the Gulf are Monhegan Sou' Sou'west, about 4 miles south-southwest of Monhegan Island; the Wall, about 10 miles east-southeast of Boothbay Harbor; Inner Kettle and Outer Kettle, 10 to 17 miles south of Seguin Island, where Captain Barry Gibson caught his 265-pound mako in 1993; and the southern tip of Mile Ledge, just below Seguin and the mouth of the Kennebec River, where Captain Ben Lewis caught a 16-foot, 450-pound thresher in 1979. Captain Matt Wilder comments, "For all-round sharking, the Kettle Ground is one of Maine's hottest spots."

Good areas for mackerel sharks include the Portland L.N.B., 8 miles east of Cape Elizabeth; The Shark Grounds, 25 miles south-southeast of the Saco River; The Gulch, 20 miles east of the mouth of the Saco, where Jim Hinkley hooked his large mako; and the area about 4 miles outside Wood Island, also at the mouth of the Saco. The rips just outside of Wood Island should interest mako hunters. Here, on Labor Day 1934, a party led by W. E. Manchester out of Biddeford Pool caught an 11-foot mako that was close to 800 pounds. The big fish, one of two spotted, was captured with a handline and a gaff made from a bent file. Not surprisingly, two more makos were seen feeding upon bluefish in the same location in 1993.

Maine's top sharking expert, Captain Cal Robinson of Saco, believes that

"anglers may be running right over productive areas like the one below Wood Island as they head out to deeper grounds." This theory of untapped mackerel-shark potential in the Gulf of Maine is corroborated by the 35-pound mako taken by Captain Pete Ripley's *Breakaway* at the 2SR buoy in the mouth of the Sheepscot River in 1993. Mate Joe Libby made a cast to the surface-finning shark, thinking it was a bluefish, and it grabbed the green and white Atom popper.

Continuing down the coast, inshore shark grounds in the southern areas include Boone Island Ledge, 15 miles east of Ogunquit; The Inner and Outer Flag, 8 miles east of the Isles of Shoals or about 16 miles southeast of Rye, New Hampshire; Old Man's Pasture, 12 miles southwest of Gloucester; and Wildcat Knoll, 25 miles east of Boston. Stellwagen Bank is accessed from Newburyport. Gloucester-Rockport, at Cape Ann; its northwestern corner is 15 miles from Eastern Point. In the 1960s, the Richard Webster family put Rockport and Stellwagen on the sharker's map with three IGFA line-class records for great blues, two of which exceeded 400 pounds. Stellwagen is only a few miles from Provincetown on Cape Cod.

Larger boats can fish the sharks out in the offshore grounds, especially a relatively untapped population of spring and fall porbeagles that also appear to winter over. With large numbers of hefty porbeagles taken in commercial gillnets in June, the species could offer excellent fishing if anglers would only try for them prior to the blue/mako season.

The Gulf of Maine's top offshore spots are Platt's Bank, 45 miles below Boothbay or 35 miles from Saco; and Jeffreys Bank, about 60 to 70 miles equidis-

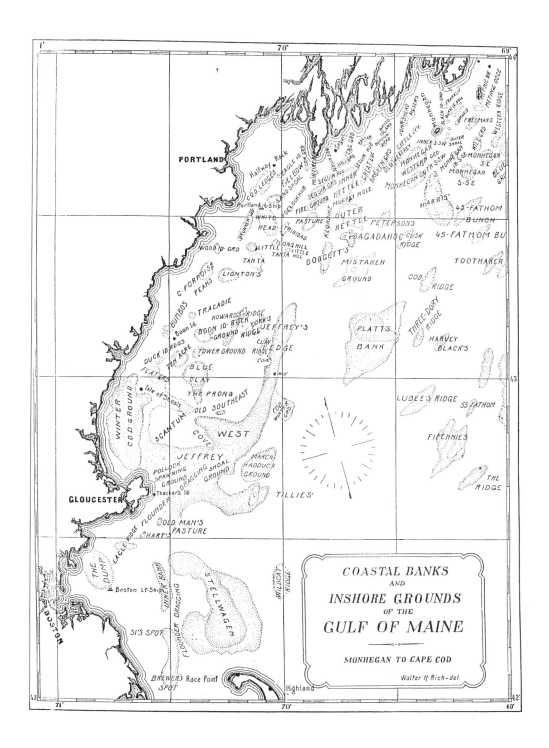

COASTAL BANKS
AND
INSHORE GROUNDS
OF THE
GULF OF MAINE

MONHEGAN TO CAPE COD

Walter H. Rich - del.

tant from Boothbay, Saco, and Portland to the east and smack in the middle of the Gulf. It has many productive banks, including the Fingers and the Outer Falls. Cashes Ledge lies Southeast 1/2S 70 miles from Portland, or 80 miles East 1/2S from Cape Ann, and runs from a breaking shoal to 50 fathoms deep. Cashes is the outermost ground accessible by sportfishermen and attracts every pelagic shark species found in New England.

To some extent, the Gulf is a "new frontier." Famous for inshore stripers and giant tuna in deeper quarters, the region receives little attention from sharkers. As they learn of its great potential, we will see more record fish taken, especially in the mackerel-shark family. We believe that the new all-tackle record mako swims in the Gulf of Maine each summer and that, sooner or later, it will come to a heavy-tackle sharker.

Southern New England

Below Cape Cod, southern New England waters have great mako potential; and blue sharks are thick in season, from late spring to early October. The outer edges of the Cape quickly drop off to deeper zones quickly. Makos pass through during the warm-water periods from mid-July to September. Bluefish, the choice of Atlantic makos everywhere, are plentiful along these ledges. Outer Crab Ledge lies 15 miles east-southeast of Chatham, Massachusetts, and its east edge drops below the 20-fathom curve. The deep drop-offs outside Nantucket Shoals attract macks, bonito, and the mackerel sharks that prey upon them. The outside edge runs north

and south for 40 miles, and Fishing Rip and Phelp's Bank lie on the 20-fathom curve 30 miles south-southeast of Nantucket Island. Care should be taken in these areas since tides run strong.

The Block Island Ground, 60 miles below Point Judith, Rhode Island, or Mystic, Connecticut, is only 10 to 30 miles southeast to southwest of Block Island. Here in 1993, Captain Andy D'Angelo's *Maridee II* took the Rhode Island state-record mako, a 10-foot, 718-pound fish caught in 64°F (18°C) water just 15 miles below the Island. The area is packed with mackerel, menhaden, and butterfish in the fall. Sharking is best from August to October. Makos and blue sharks are often located along the 40-fathom curve, or the 43600 loran line that runs east-west.

The Mid-Atlantic Coast

Montauk, on the east end of Long Island, New York, is the most famous sharking port in the Northeast and the home of Frank Mundus, noted for catching the largest fish taken on rod and reel—a 3,427-pound great white. From here, sharkers swing around Montauk's Lighthouse Point and find excellent fishing, often close to the beach for sandbar sharks since the Island's south-shore inlets attract browns entering the shallows to feed from early June through the summer.

Duskies are taken offshore, often in less than 20 fathoms; and deeper waters hold blue sharks and makos in numbers, the latter arriving in mid-June and remaining until the end of July, and then passing through again during September and October. Makos are often caught on the Butterfish Hole, 40 miles

Francis Low, an early East Coast big-game angler (c. 1930), with his record-setting, 998-pound, Atlantic great white, taken outside of Mannisquam Inlet. This Ashaway Line Co. photo was retouched to remove the shark's large gut; the new look conforms to the sleek lines of popular billfish.

Al Ristori

The grounds off Montauk, Long Island, are perhaps the best known shark waters in the United States. Captain Al Ristori displays a nice mako, which will be invited to a barbecue.

Jersey's south shore, and incidental catches are made from July to mid-September. Brown sharks, ideal for small craft, arrive in late spring and stay throughout the summer off the inlets at Shark River, Mannisquam, Barnagat, Little Egg, Great Egg, and Cape May, which are dotted with marinas that host large summertime flotillas of sportfishermen. The boats venture offshore, where migrating blue sharks are found in June and early July.

From Cape May to the Outer Banks of North Carolina, hundreds of inlets and jetties offer an inshore sharker the opportunity to pick up ground sharks. As the center of this region, Chesapeake Bay is also the northernmost reach of many tropical sharks. The eastern shore of the Chesapeake sees a number of sand tigers and inshore requiems in the spring. Chesapeake's western shore runs to open beaches, and we have seen tigers feeding upon small chopper bluefish off Damn Neck beach. The 17 Mile Bridge offers sand tigers; but the better areas are inside the Bay, where deep channels and slopes hold duskies all summer long. Some of the top dusky spots include the North Channel, King's Creek Channel, and The Cigar. Offshore, blue sharks pass by in May on their way north.

Experienced sharker Wayne McNamee notes that the Chesapeake is a pupping ground for requiems frequenting the area and that gravid fish should be released with care during the spring. Most species will remain throughout the summer, but the blues and makos stay outside of Cape Henry–Cape Charles, moving rapidly northward as the seas warm until they reach Jersey waters. The Maryland–Delaware leg of the migration lasts for just over a week.

Years ago, the Virginia Beach Shark

east-southeast of Shinnecock Inlet, and at Forty Fathom Fingers, 45 miles south-southeast of Shinnecock. The 210 Lump, 30 miles southeast of Lighthouse Point, holds makos, blue sharks, and occasional threshers. The great whites, made famous by Mr. Mundus, are never plentiful but arrive with the pilot whales, remaining from mid-June to the end of August.

Threshers are always rare but are taken from Long Island down to New

Club patrolled the surf in specialized buggies with outriggers. They used heavy tackle and took some impressive catches. Today beach "trolling" has been discontinued because the inshore shark population has dwindled and anglers are more release-oriented. On North Carolina's Outer Banks, occasional sand tigers are still hooked at Oregon Inlet by surf anglers fishing bait for other species.

Inside Pamlico Sound, a variety of sharks are found when temperature conditions are right. Large bull sharks have been caught in Pamlico's shallows, and huge lemons up to 300 pounds cruise through in the spring and in September. Many locally caught lemons have stomachs full of stingray horns.

Open waters outside of Pamlico, from Hatteras to Ocracoke, hold makos during the winter and early spring. Anglers who drift the 35-fathom curve will find makos in cooler zones around 64 to 68°F (18 to 20°C), and tigers in water 72 to 73°F (22 to 23°C). The tigers remain throughout the summer. Anglers will find the 100-fathom curve is only 25 miles from inlets. The Gulf Stream wends close to shore here; only outside of Palm Beach Inlet in Florida can you get closer to it. Good depths close to land, combined with water that reaches tropical temperatures, account for the variety of southern species in the area. In late spring, when surface temperatures push above the low 70-degree mark, the cold-water sharks move north. The best time for mako angling is January and February.

Captain Berle Wilson, aboard his *Good Times* out of Hatteras, has taken a number of prized sharks through the years. "More than structure, it's the conditions and water temperature," he cautions. Anglers will find accessible sharking from

Hatteras Inlet. Good grounds include the area 7 miles out, between the Inlet and the Hook; The Dixie Arrow, 16 miles to the southeast; The Slick Stink Wreck, 16 to 17 miles southeast; and The Rock Pile, about 22 miles south-southeast of the Inlet. The Point, 35 miles north of Diamond Shoals, is noted for big tigers, and sharks are plentiful there during the king-mackerel season.

Rick West, a commercial shark fisherman from Frisco, mentions a top offshore mako spot that can be productive from December to March, located 10 to 12 miles northeast of Frying Pan Shoals and about 45 miles off Cape Fear. (Be warned that Cape Fear gets its name from the nasty water that churns across the area in stormy weather.)

Below Cape Fear, sand tigers can be found at the entrance to Pine Island Cut in South Carolina. Blacktips feed along the edges of the channels at many outfalls from Hatteras south. Blacktips will also follow shrimp boats. South Carolina shark anglers find sand tigers over a number of inshore artificial reefs, such as Paradise Reef, 3.2 miles east-southeast from the tip of the South Murrells Inlet jetty, and Little River Reef, 2.7 miles east-southeast of Little River's south jetty. In the summer, duskies and tigers are taken off St. Helena Sound.

Deeper offshore spots include Ten Mile Reef, 9½ miles southeast of the Murrells Inlet south jetty; Capers Reef, bearing 12 miles due east of the Charleston jetties; and Edisto Offshore Reef, 23.5 miles south-southeast of Stono Inlet and one of the deepest at 70 feet. The old ferry *City of Richmond* lies in 50 feet of water about 14 miles southeast of the Winyah Bay jetty, marked by buoy WR2A. These offshore areas are shallow, and pelagic sharks rarely visit them. Coastal requiems will hang around the reefs, many of which have trolling alleys for king fishermen, so do not anchor in these access ways. A few offshore sharks come in close, and a 406-pound bigeye thresher was taken off Edisto Island.

The Southeast

The region from Georgia down to the Florida Keys provides a multitude of southern species. Just outside of Savannah Harbor, sand tigers are taken off the outside drop-offs of the Savannah Tower. Like South Carolina, Georgia has natural reefs far out to sea, and most accessible offshore reefs are manmade. The reefs are supplemented by several U.S. Navy aircraft training towers 30 to 40 miles offshore.

Inshore anglers are far luckier; the low-lying areas from the Altamaha River to Florida's St. Johns River are a mass of snaking waterways and sounds within barrier islands. This is prime shallow-water sharking territory, with lemons and other tropical inshore species rooting for benthic food at Altamaha, St. Simons, St. Mary, St. Andrew, and Nassau Sounds.

To date, this potentially important estuarine system has been ignored by sharkers. In July and August, when water temperatures reach 78 to 84°F (26 to 29°C), lemons and blacktips should move into the sounds, flats, and river mouths, offering light-tackle action to those who know the sharks are there.

St. Johns River, the end of the sea-island stretch, and the Fernandina Inlet submarine channel hold ground sharks. At St. Johns, the Florida coastline becomes the archetypal fun-in-the-sun beach terrain, and so it continues south to Biscayne Bay— a good area for hammerheads in the spring.

Offshore, from Daytona Beach to Fort Pierce, the continental shelf finally moves closer, and drop-offs plunge to 100 fathoms or more at 30 to 40 miles from the inlets. Just inside the shelf, spires rise toward the surface, peaking at 250 to 280 feet. Called *cones,* they cause upwellings that bring nutrients to the upper strata. One cone is located at loran TDs 43862.3/61806.3, just 29 miles from Port Canaveral. Hammerheads, makos, and even whites are taken there from December to the end of April. Spring anglers can fish the 35- to 50-fathom lines for little tunny, and use them as live bait in the same area for tigers. Or move a tad inshore where ground sharks have an amazing ability to find a baitfish in distress. We've hooked sharks off Palm Beach Inlet using this technique.

From Biscayne Bay to Key West, South Florida waters are dotted with cays and flats, producing classic conditions for inshore shark angling with light tackle. The Florida flats hold sharks year-round, but the highest concentrations of inshore requiems are found during the warmer, summer months. Late-winter sharking is also good just outside the flats, and a center-console boat is ideal for the job.

The Florida Straits along the eastern side of the Keys sees excellent deep-water action in September and October, and again in April and May. Heidi Mason's massive 463-pound hammerhead was a spring Keys fish. The Humps are top offshore sharking spots in this area. Located in the Gulf Stream off the Middle Keys, 12 to 25 miles out, they hold late-fall and winter makos, and big tigers and hammerheads year-round. Ascending from depths of almost 170 fathoms, these sea mounts peak at 83 fathoms below the surface. The Islamorada Hump (14098.5/43266.5), 14 miles from that Key, is the most popular.

Bad dog-day shark. As an early sportfishing center, even Miami had slow days. This 1937 catch included several half-eaten "bonito," an amberjack, two barracuda, and this tortured and strangled ground shark.

Other grounds include Marathon Hump (14032.5/43358.6), out from that Key; the 409 Hump, almost 20 miles from Lower Matacumbe Key; and the West Hump, just over 23 miles from Duck Key. Sharkers who fish the Humps use heavy tackle, and Dacron line is a good idea in these great depths because it doesn't stretch, which facilitates hookup. Big baits, amberjack taken on the grounds, are lowered into the depths during a drift. Currents are strong, and boat repositioning is required every 20 minutes. Baits have been swallowed by monster sharks, including great whites; the largest was a 1,130-pounder taken by Captain Bob Taunte's *Jeri-Lyn*.

Just off Florida's east coast, the Bahamas bask in the Gulf Stream. At Bimini, now famous for a knot, Papa Hemingway took a long-standing-record Atlantic mako. He didn't think much of sharks, however, and used a Thompson submachine gun to pepper them with lead. The God of Sharks, the Great Manasharka, took revenge on Ernie: One day when Hemingway was blasting away, he somehow managed to shoot himself in the foot. He was forced to recuperate at the Complete Angler; and if his stay was anything like ours, he drifted off to sleep each night to the strains of lullabies played by a very loud calypso band in the bar downstairs.

The Gulf of Mexico

Shark fishing from the Gulf side of Florida to Texas can be even more exciting than Hemingway's style, yet very few anglers give it a try. The shores of the Gulf of Mexico are shallow and sandy, with barrier islands sprinkled down to Mexico's Yucatán Peninsula. This is prime hammerhead, blacktip, spinner, and dusky-shark country, as all species venture close to shore. Tigers are also taken, but they're getting rare. Many Gulf sharkers cast light tackle from the beaches, targeting junior members of those species. Others fish over natural, offshore hard-bottom or coral structure as well as off local inlets, often at night.

During nocturnal forays, skiff fishermen should refrain from hanging tail-roped sharks overboard. In June 1991, while sharking in Florida's Chassahowitzka Bay, Captain Dennis Royston of Hudson had a moonlight visit from a shark as long as his 16-foot flats skiff. It swallowed the better part of a 6-footer that was hanging over the side, then spun the boat in circles and nearly swamped it.

Offshore areas account for most of the heavy sharks in the eastern Gulf. In Alabama, Orange Beach is a prime central location. Although the port is famous for snappers, sharking rates high. As in most other parts of the globe, longliners are targeting the local species, and the shark pop-

Gulf Coast sharking can range from light-tackle species along the barrier islands to offshore brutes, such as this 990-pound tiger, the current Alabama state record.

John E. Phillips

ulation is not as high as it was a decade ago. The Orange Beach Marina Monster Shark Tournament now imposes a 100-inch limit on entries.

Captain Barry Ingram, skipper of the *Reel Lucky,* has been sharking from the area for 20 years, and on a good day he can still hook an average of three requiems or hammerheads, which are tagged and released. He believes in fishing natural structure rather than wrecks and off the mouths of inlets and bays during the outgoing tides. Ingram likes bonito and jacks for baits, fishing them 8 feet deep and right next to bottom.

Summertime sharking is also good at the entrance of Mobile Bay; and just west and outside, Alabama's Dauphin Island and Mississippi's Petit Bois and Horn Islands offer light-tackle sharking from late spring until fall. These barrier islands are accessible by boat from Pascagoula and from Biloxi and Gulfport, Mississippi. During June and July, chum can be purchased from the shrimpers that move into the area.

Venice and Port Eads, on Louisiana's Delta and well below New Orleans, offer a demarcation point to offshore sharking. From the mouth of South Pass at the Delta tip, the 100-fathom curve is about 10 miles distant. There is no reason to venture that far out, since the 40- and 50-fathom curves hold sharks wherever there's structure. Deeper waters can also be accessed from Port Arthur, Texas.

The Barrier Islands pick up again west of Port Arthur and stretch to Port Isabel at the Mexican border. This is prime small-requiem country, productive from spring until late fall. After the cold fronts hit in October, the sharks seek deeper channels but move into shallows during the midday sun. Until the surface temperatures drop below 70°F (21°C), sharks are taken along these 400 miles of outer-island surf. Port O'Connor is a good central location for working the south shores of the islands, and even the jetties produce fish.

The top sport sharks are blacktips, but there are also sharpnose, bonnetheads, bull-itas (little bulls), and silky sharks. Individuals are small and sporty on light tackle, but a lot of anglers use standard East Coast–style surf rods, 9 to 10 feet long. In years past, Texas sharkers fished the beaches at night for huge hammerheads

Abe Cuanang

Sevengills are primitive sharks that inhabit the depths, yet they are targeted and regularly taken in San Francisco Bay.

and prized tigers until angling started to decline. Monster sharks still pass through, so remember to gear up a little heavier for nocturnal sharks.

Central California Hot Spots

California offers some of the best light-tackle mako and blue-shark angling in the country, and a growing thresher fishery is tapping an old sport fish with new vigor. Coastal sharks are also available: leopard sharks, soupfins, and the ancient seven- and sixgill sharks.

The promotion of sevengill fishing

can be credited in part to expert anglers Abe and Angelo Cuanang. Fishing the depths of San Francisco Harbor, they have taken fish up to 300 pounds. Sevengills are found in 70 to 100 feet of water; the largest individuals have been taken at the area called Raccoon Straits between Tiburon and Angel Islands, on the east side of Angel Island, and on the west side of Alcatraz Island. Abe's favorite spot is the deep drop-off north of Marin's Yellow Bluff.

The peak season runs from August to October. Heavy currents warrant substantial tackle, and 3-pound ball sinkers are used to get the bait to bottom. Most anglers use downrigger cable for line and rods equipped with hard rollers, but the new Kevlar lines may present another option.

The inner Bay area also has excellent leopard-shark fishing, sometimes in water as shallow as 40 to 60 feet along the channel edges. Angling peaks in the spring and can be good from spring through fall. Leopards can be found throughout the Bay system from northern San Pablo Bay to the southern extreme at Dumbarton Bridge. Excellent grounds are located south of San Rafael Bridge, west of Alcatraz Island, east of Angel Island, and just south of the San Francisco Oakland Bay Bridge off Mission Rock. Herring and squid are good baits, but the best offerings are springtime midshipmen.

Most of those spots hold active soupfins as well. Their preferred baits are squid, chunks of salmon, or a combo of the two; they will also grab a live midshipman. Soupfins, heavily fished commercially for fins and formerly for oil, are trying to make a comeback. Release as many as possible. The best tides for all Bay species are the last few hours of the rush toward high and the immediate ebb. In fact, that's a good time of the tide to fish for sharks anywhere in the world.

The Central California area also offers good deep-water angling for blue sharks. Although they normally frequent humps on the 100-fathom line, some venture closer to shore. Abe Cuanang notes, "Blue sharks are targeted by only a handful of light-tackle specialists and fly-rodders during the late summer and early fall, when offshore conditions can be very mild."

Whalers can be found off Point Reyes, especially just outside of Cordell Bank. To the south and 27 miles west of San Francisco, the famous Farallon Islands Reserve holds the majestic great white and sizable packs of blues. The requiems skirt the perimeter of the Islands along the many reefs. Even more blues will be found west of the Farallons and farther southwest on the 100-fathom marks. Here, active shearwaters and chick birds indicate schools of squid and sauries, with the great blues hanging below.

Continuing south, blues can be located outside of Half Moon Bay on the Deep Reef, and well outside on the Guide and Pioneer Seamounts.

Southern California

Makos are the most popular sharks in Southern California, where anglers are very enthusiastic about these acrobatic fish. For reasons not yet fathomed, most California makos are small, usually under 100 pounds and 35 to 65 pounds on average. The California Bight at Point Conception is the northernmost range of these fish, and many sharkers believe that the area from Santa Catalina to San Clemente Islands and San Diego is a pup-rearing ground. Now that commercial netting has been banned in these waters, the mako population is

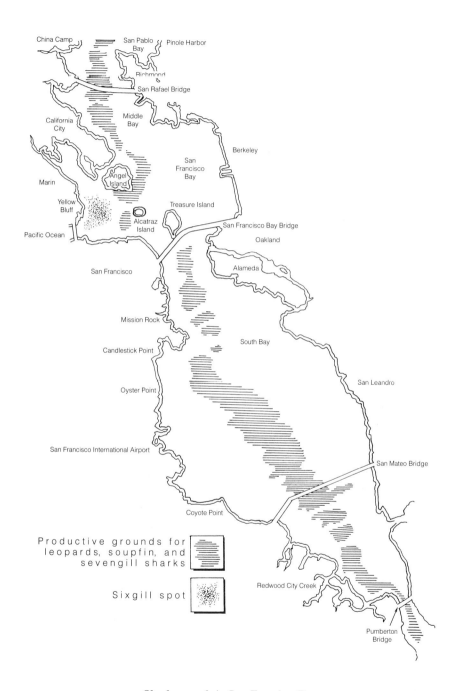

China Camp
San Pablo Bay
Pinole Harbor
Richmond
San Rafael Bridge
Middle Bay
California City
Berkeley
San Francisco Bay
Marin
Angel Island
Yellow Bluff
Treasure Island
Alcatraz Island
Pacific Ocean
San Francisco Bay Bridge
Oakland
San Francisco
Alameda
Mission Rock
South Bay
Candlestick Point
Oyster Point
San Leandro
San Francisco International Airport
San Mateo Bridge
Coyote Point
Redwood City Creek
Pumberton Bridge

Productive grounds for
leopards, soupfin, and
sevengill sharks

Sixgill spot

Shark grounds in San Francisco Bay.

increasing—great news for the sportfishing crowd.

Captain Beak Hurt, an expert billfish and sharking skipper living in Carlsbad, is on the mako grounds whenever he gets the opportunity. His advice on chum: "If I'm going for makos, I want nothing but fish scent." He also scans the surface and skies while running to a mark. If activity is present, even if it's short of the peaks, "The Beak" will slow-troll the area.

This high population of small California makos is best fished from May to November, the warmer months. During the winter the fish move off into water over 100 fathoms, and anglers must contend with a long run and greater depths. When the waters reach mid-60 temperatures (about 18°C), local mako anglers drift and slow-troll and also carry a rigged casting rod for surface-finners or free-jumpers.

Some of the best areas are 14 Mile Bank, a 50-fathom submerged mount located 11 miles, 210°, out of Dana Point Harbor and southwest of Newport Beach; the 279, about 10 miles east of the 14 Mile Bank; and The Slide, due east of Santa Catalina and about 26 miles out of Dana Point. Just east of The Slide, on the area called The Ridge, is a productive mark called the 277 Spot. The 209, just south-southwest of the 279, is another good Ridge area; and Avalon Bank, just east of The Slide, is a popular spot for sharks.

The Slide attracts quantities of Pacific green macks and the blue sharks and makos that feed upon them. The Ridge cuts a 30-mile-long area of broken bottom and peaks at 140 fathoms starting just 20 miles west of Point Loma and San Diego. A few larger makos of up to 300 pounds are taken each year on these banks, and fish of 1,000 pounds have been sighted;

Dave Elm

Southern California has a good thresher population and is perhaps the only area in the United States where the species can be taken in a directed sportfishery.

but the whereabouts of the population of monster fish has yet to be discovered.

Most of these banks also hold active threshers. The 181 and 182 are located about 30 miles off San Diego. The Mackerel Bank off San Clemente and the 125 Spot off the west end of Catalina are also good. Aftco's Dave Elm adds sage advice on the intermix of makos, threshers, and billfish: "A lot of guys, some commercial, do well in the channel between the west end of Catalina and Point Vincente, a spot on the chart called The Boot. Always carry a marlin casting rod and a swordfish casting rod. All these areas can produce these species if the conditions are right. Also, you should always carry live bait. Take the time to make mackerel because these species (including makos and threshers) are all aggressive and prefer live bait."

Threshers are becoming plentiful and are often big, in excess of 200 pounds. The highest angling effort has been in the Santa Monica Bay area, where since 1977 no less than eight world line-class records have been established. Virtually every IGFA record thresher taken on 8- to 20-lb test was caught in the area from the Catalina Channel south to Point Vincente. Sometimes the fish are taken close to shore, and some have been caught just 2 to 5 miles off South Laguna Beach, the landmarks being Aliso Pier or Laguna Hospital just north of Dana Point.

Many fishermen prefer to slow-troll with 50-lb-class tackle, which is heavy for most makos but offers a better chance of landing the larger threshers. What's a great day in California waters? Dave Elm capped a recent trip with six threshers and two makos, releasing all but two threshers, one

of which weighed 236 pounds. Dave is an itinerant thresher buff and comments: "Another great aspect to thresher fishing is that, once hooked, they jump. They dive deep in the beginning of the fight like a swordfish; then toward the end they act like big tuna and go into their death spiral, circling as you bring them up. The sheer size of these creatures is awesome." Considering that local commercials have taken threshers up to 800 pounds, the sport-angling sector has some potential heavyweights to strive for in the future.

A final note and story from Dave Elm: "Threshers can be found in all water conditions. We have our greatest success in off-green water. Last year (1993) while trolling for marlin in the 277 spot, we saw a fin behind one of the jigs. Well, it turned out not to be a fin at all but the tail of a 200-plus thresher. This fish was actually trying to slap the marlin jig with its tail." Dave hauled in the billfish lures and slow-trolled the area with live bait; after ten minutes the downrigger went off. "I don't think it was the same fish because it seemed quite a bit smaller—only 150 pounds. The point is when you see life, especially the type you are looking for, stop and put a bait in the water because you can't catch sharks without a wet line."

11

SHARKING

Mrs. Joyce Yallop with her 500-pound mako, which was for many years the largest rod-and-reel shark taken off the British coast.

SACGB

WORLDWIDE

Along the edge of the western Atlantic, from Canada to South America, the sharks are waiting. In the eastern Atlantic, the British Isles offer tope and the best porbeagle marks on the globe. And in the South Pacific, Australia has traditionally produced the world's finest white- and tiger-shark angling. Surrounded by temperate waters, New Zealand boasts the largest of the threshers, consistent makos, and great light-tackle tope fishing.

Near-Virgin Canadian Waters

Even in the coldest regions of the North Atlantic, like the St. Lawrence River in Quebec, shark anglers find sporting species. Here, in midwinter, Greenland sharks are captured through the ice. It is a herculean task to handline 300 pounds of fish up from the frigid depths, but a small group of dedicated Canadians brave subzero temperatures to bait their quarry.

The Gulf of St. Lawrence offers summer shark waters yet untapped, and areas such as the Magdalen Islands have the right temperatures, baitfish, and structure to attract porbeagles. Likewise, the northern and southern coasts of Prince Edward Island hold temperate sharks that feed on capelin, northern ballyhoo, and the schools of large mackerel found there.

Nova Scotia has so far seen limited shark sportfishing, but some of the best spring porbeagle grounds in the Bay of Fundy can be accessed from Yarmouth, as well as Campobello Island on the New Brunswick side. And the Atlantic side of Nova Scotia has very good blue sharking during the summer. Recently, a great white supposedly weighing more than a ton became entangled in a commercial fisherman's net and was towed into Halifax.

Mexico to South America

The Caribbean side of Yucatán is characterized by deep-water ports like Cancún, on the mainland, and the isle of Cozumel. This is a spectacular billfishing area, and locals

Ray Barry

*A large scalloped hammerhead caught by Joe "Kastaway" Kulis off the mouth
of the Rio Colorado on the Caribbean coast of Costa Rica.*

view sharkers as somewhat odd. Nonetheless, some big tigers are taken as incidental catches, showing the presence of tropical requiems. Belize, south of the Peninsula, has a network of coral reefs and flats where hammerheads and blacktips cruise.

From Belize, along the Mosquito Coast, down to Costa Rica, the small requiems and hammerheads are joined by populations of bull and lemon sharks. Anglers looking for light-tackle records will have their best shot in the estuarine areas of Nicaragua and Costa Rica. There are large numbers of bull sharks along the 30- to 40-fathom line outside the Rio San Juan to the

Rio Parismina; at the entrances of those two rivers, the Rio Colorado, and the Rio Tortuguero; and along the outer river bars. Famous for ascending the Rio San Juan, the *toro grande* (great bull) travels hundreds of miles upriver to Lake Nicaragua.

Bull sharks are feared in this region, for good cause, and they are also eaten by the coastal villagers they prey upon. Local fishermen in dugout canoes motor seaward and set anchored lines attached to a large buoy. They catch not only bulls but hammerheads and big lemon sharks, whose packs can be large in the spring. A sport angler equipped with chum will find the area holds the greatest number of sharks in Central America.

On the Pacific side of Mexico just below California, the long Baja Peninsula extends southward to Cabo San Lucas. Anglers have caught makos on the Pacific side as well as in the mouth of the Gulf of California, which is accessible from Cabo, the East Cape, and Mazatlán on the main. This area also holds hammerheads in the warmer months.

We have baited hammerheads while billfishing out of Mazatlán and farther south at Barra de Navidad. From October to March, the fish will be outside in the warmer blue water. At Ixtapa hammerheads are also common inshore during the summer. In the winter the fish move off to waters roughly about 100 miles out, yet dedicated commercial panga fishermen

make the journey and bring home the meat. Out of San Jose, Guatemala, panga fishermen shoot long distances to take soupfins, which are dry-salted and sold to the Mexican market.

Off Cabo Marzo and Bahia Solero, Colombia, we have found hammerheads very close to shore in May. Cabo Marzo's waters are deep and blue within a half mile of shore, teeming with small tuna, and the hammerheads are right with them.

Great Britain

In the eastern Atlantic, off the shores of Cornwall, Wales, and Scotland, British anglers fish for porbeagles, tope, blue sharks, and the rare mako. They are very serious about sharking, having developed techniques that American anglers are just

Chris Bennett

The largest porbeagle caught in the North, Chris Bennett's 507-pounder also stands as the IGFA all-tackle record for the species.

learning. Sharkers are a special breed, and the fish we seek are our common ground— on both sides of the "Pond."

The Gulf Stream's North Atlantic Drift feeds warm water to the West Country, providing a comfort zone for blue sharks and tope. Even a few threshers are taken each year from mildly temperate zones in the South. Cold-water areas in the East and far North provide year-round angling for record-size porbeagles, particularly in the north of Scotland, where an excellent mackerel sharkery is just beginning as new marks are located.

The Eastern Channel

Without the warming effect of the North Atlantic Drift, the waters around the Isle of Wight host but two species, porbeagles and threshers. Around the south side of the Isle, porbeagles arrive in late May and usually remain until September's end. The fish run in packs, congregating in a small area while the waters around them may appear to be lifeless. Captain Ted Legg says that it can sometimes be difficult to locate the sharks since they're so tightly concentrated in a 1,600-square-mile area but that, once a pack is located, catches of better than 10 fish a day are possible.

Top ports for hitting this fishery are Portsmouth on the mainland and Bembridge on the Isle of Wight. Anglers may also run into a thresher now and then. As the European record skipper for the species, Ted informs us that "Threshers are spread throughout the area, and each appears to have its own territory. It is possible to target a particular fish on the basis of reported sightings of the thresher shark free-jumping, but remember he is a cunning adversary. Just because you know

where the shark is, it does not always mean you can inspire him to strike a bait."

As Captain Legg implies, eastern Channel sharking can be difficult, but the rewards can be great. The best baits are live mackerel fished in a mackerel chum slick; when the bait is no longer active, it should be changed.

The West Country of England

With the introduction of "Rubby Dubby" in 1952, the West Country became the first region to cultivate a blue shark sportfishery. Brigadier J. A. L. Caunter, an early proponent of sharking out of Looe, founded the Shark Angling Club of Great Britain in 1953 with 12 members. With the growth of the organization, the SACGB popularized the sport; they now keep the official British line-class and all-tackle shark records. Blue sharks average 60 to 70 pounds; and the standing British record fish, at 218 pounds, was caught by Nigel Sutcliffe in 1959. The waters around Cornwall and Devon still attract numbers of blue sharks along the 35- to 40-fathom marks some 20 to 25 miles offshore. The season can start as early as March and runs until October, peaking from early June to the end of September. Besides Looe, ports include Penzance, Falmouth, Fowey, Mevagissey, and Plymouth to the south.

British sharker Chris Sinclair has followed the mako successes in the West Country and notes, "The mako shark has always been something of a mystery. . . . Totally unpredictable, this fish can turn up anywhere, although reefs such as The Manacles off Falmouth and Wolf Rock out towards the Isles of Scilly offer the best potential." In the past decade or so, sport-caught mako catches have declined to the point that a catch is now considered quite an achievement. Actually, for large mako sharks that's true worldwide.

The original catch for the species was set at Looe in 1955 by Mrs. Hetty Eathorne. This mako weighed 352 pounds and was initially thought to be a porbeagle. Not the first or last unintentional "fako" (as Maine's Captain Cal Robinson once said), Mrs. Eathorne's fish was properly identified when it was submitted as a world record. It became the first rod-and-reel mako of official British record. Several other notable makos were taken at Looe, and Mr. K. Wilson's 428½-pounder pushed the record higher in 1961.

A decade later, the charter boat *Lady Betty* sighted what Captain A. Dingle

thought was a basking shark finning on the surface off Eddystone Reef, 13 miles south of Plymouth. Upon closer inspection, the basker turned out to be a large mako. The fish was baited and hooked, and the angler, Mrs. Joyce Yallop of Norwich, successfully fought the mako for three and a half hours before it came to gaff. Landed at Looe's SACGB Headquarters, the shark topped the scales at 500 pounds and still stands as the British mako record.

Just to the north, the ports of Bude and Padstow offer access to some of the best porbeagle angling in the West Country. Located just below the entrance to the Bristol Channel, Padstow boasts seven line-class world records for that species. Until March of 1993, Jorge Potier's locally caught 465-pounder held the all-tackle world

Simon Williams

Simon Williams holds a 38-pound Welsh tope, taken on 15-lb-test line in June 1993.

record. The best mark is Crackington Haven, just north of Padstow and a few miles off the coast. Sinclair describes its structure as jagged pinnacles of rock just below the surface—ideal porbeagle country.

The local porgies frequent shallower depths than blue sharks and are taken year-round. The prime angling months are from May to September, when the seas of Crackington Haven are generally calmer. The fish remain throughout the winter months as well, but the run of the tide and rough water make angling difficult.

Threshers are infrequent but welcome catches in the West. The first rod-and-reel thresher catch in Cornwall, Brigadier Caunter's 268-pounder, was made in 1959. Caunter related, "This was caught at Looe . . . with pollack bait and the boat at anchor on a rock mark." The current British record fish, at 323 pounds, was taken off the Isle of Wight in 1982, but a commercial trawler netted a 600-plus-pounder at Looe in 1993. With these sharks, the best bait is a live one. An abundance of local mackerel and pilchards makes ideal thresher fodder, also attracting the porbeagles and blues. These sharks also feed on benthic pollack and coalfish. With its ideal water temperatures, the Devon-Cornwall region will remain one of Great Britain's top sharking areas.

Wales

Continuing up the western coast, we find Cardigan Bay with its porbeagles, a lesser population of blues, and tope. For tope, however, Wales's little Caernarvon Bay produces one of the best fisheries in Britain. Located in the Irish Sea just above Cardigan, Caernarvon is ideal for small craft. Tides are light, and the tope can be located

in less than 50 feet of water. According to Simon Williams, this is ideal light-tackle territory. Boats are launched at Caernarvon, Rhosneigr (on Anglesey), and farther down the Bay at Trevor. The fish are "fairly catholic feeders," and Williams, who has fished the Bay since 1986, has taken tope on herring, pollack, and garfish. The staple is mackerel, which are freelined whole in depths of 25 feet or less. In deeper waters, a standard running ledger is used. Light-tackle anglers rate tope higher in fightability than blue sharks, and use 12- to 15-lb-test gear. An average fish weighs about 30 pounds, and a few top 40 pounds; they max out at 50.

As for setting the hook on tope, Williams warns us that "Bites range from the standard shark-type run followed by a pause (when the fish turns the bait in its mouth), after which the fish should be struck, to slack-line bites caused by the fish running towards the boat; these should be struck as soon as contact with the fish is established."

Scotland's New Frontier

Above Caernarvon Bay, the Irish Sea extends beyond the Isle of Man and Solway Firth, finally meeting the North Channel. We are in Scottish waters now, a true "new frontier" in the world of shark angling.

Sharking was not a high priority among Scots until the very late 1980s, when a few anglers realized that their local waters held some weighty mackerel sharks. Early in 1989 the Big Game Club of Scotland was formed, and during the past five years, Club members have taken some of the most impressive winter porbeagles ever caught. During this short period the BGCS has compiled a detailed data bank of the porbeagle's seasonal movements, based on both rod-and-reel and commercial catches.

Stan Massey, one of the most active of the Club's founding members, has intimate knowledge of the porbeagle's meanderings: "The west coast of Scotland sees a northern migration of porbeagle into coastal waters in mid-May, and this migration can be tracked north from Mull of Galloway, Irish Sea area, in May and spreading rapidly north to the Western Isles and northwest coast by around September."

This movement coincides with the migration of shoals (schools) of mackerel, scad, and herring. Since grounds off the Western Isles may hold large porbeagles, the BGCS is fitting out a new long-range, 50-foot sportfisherman for the next summer season.

Throughout Scottish waters, porbeagles travel in packs as they do in other parts of the United Kingdom. The east-coast fish are most numerous off the estuaries of the Rivers Forth, Tay, Dee, and Don from July through September. These are also the months of the traditional Atlantic salmon runs into these eastern rivers. Stan Massey believes this is not just a coincidence but that the porbeagles are in hot pursuit of the salmon. All mackerel sharks have an affinity for oily fish, and salmon may be high on their list of favorites.

The angling successes along the east coast of Scotland are actually surpassed by an excellent winter sport fishery in the North. Incidental catches of porbeagles are made during the winter months elsewhere (notably in the West of England and in Maine, where 18 Kettle Bottom fish were once gillnetted by the *Casey-Ann* two days before Christmas); but Scottish packs are numerous, and individual fish are huge.

The BGCS members theorize that

porbeagles cruising northward after mackerel and herring intercept the beginning of the shoreward cod migration, which moves into the northern coast to spawn beginning in late September and early October. The availability of cod ("easy food") holds the porbeagle packs until March, long after the mackerel have headed south. Massey

BGCS

A 50-lb-class IGFA record fish, Rob Richardson's porbeagle was taken on stand-up tackle off Dunnet Head, northern Scotland.

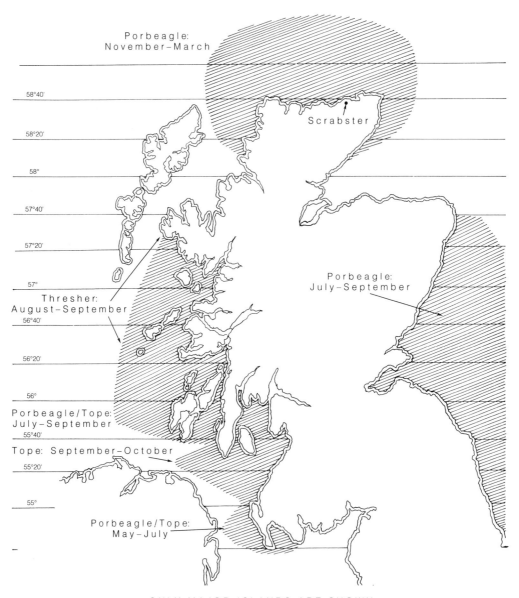

The shark grounds of Scotland.

comments, "Certainly the largest shark[s] have been contacted in midwinter off the northern coastline. . . . The headlands of the Pentland Firth in the far North of Scotland have witnessed many epic struggles between angler and porbeagle since the BGCS first experimented in these waters in the winter of 1990."

The publicity officer for the Sport-fishing Club of the British Isles, Dave Sneath, is so impressed with the North's recent record-toppling porgies that he says, "In my opinion this will be the most exciting shark fishery in the world in the not too distant future. Even in the limited time they [the Scots] have been exploring up there, they have busted a couple of world records, and there are a lot more on their way I promise you."

At present a smattering of converted commercial vessels tap the winter angling in the small port of Scrabster. Aboard Captain Sinclair Calder's *Karen*, which started out as a seinenetter, two impressive new IGFA records were taken exactly a year apart. In March of 1992, Rob Richardson tied into a chunky 414-pound porgy off Dunnet Head. At the same location Chris Bennett broke the IGFA all-tackle and 500-pound mark with a fish that also holds the Scottish, British, European, and world 80-lb-class title. Chris took his fish on a 3-pound live coalfish and says, "Conditions were interesting with a 6-meter swell and 6 knots of tide, and the fish took 2¼ hours to beat." Many other heavyweights have been captured between November and March, including several porbeagles in the 200-pound range and one 350-pounder.

Blue sharks and rare hammerheads are among the other species present in Scottish waters. Since the North Atlantic current passes down to the west, this could also turn out to be mako country. Tope are thick along the west coast from early May until late October and early November. "The whereabouts of tope can be pin-pointed to the week as they move north from Mull of Galloway in May, reaching the Isle of Skye waters in August. A southern return journey sees sport continue in reverse right through October," reports Stan Massey. Smaller tope of 15 to 30 pounds are the first to arrive in the area, followed by larger individuals that often exceed 60 pounds. The heaviest fish of the 1993 season, a 68-pounder, was taken by David McNair off the Isle of Mull. At present, the Scots are releasing their sport-caught tope, and the BGCS has instituted two shark-tagging programs.

The purely Scottish sharking scene is carried out very close to land. Winter porbeagles at Scrabster are taken in less than 150 feet of water, sometimes within 200 yards of shore. The same applies to threshers and tope in the West, and blue sharks are taken along the 100-fathom marks just 4 miles out. In the Irish Sea and some Western Isles, the pelagic areas are about 6 to 8 miles offshore, where depths can reach 150 fathoms.

In the future, these regions will produce good blue sharking, especially if Rubby Dubby is tried. Blue sharks, the garbage pails of the Atlantic, will sniff up through a slick faster than any other species, including tuna. As of this writing, this use of chum, or "berley," is not popular, but the major sport-fishery has been for porbeagle sharks, which so often feed by sight and by baitfish distress signals. Scotland's mackerel- and requiem-shark fisheries are obviously healthy, and in the future even more British and international records will be broken.

Australia

We automatically associate Australia with great whites since more record whites have been taken Down Under than any place else on the globe. The 1950s saw phenomenal catches at the old Tangalooma Whaling Station in Moretown Bay, just below the southern end of the Great Barrier Reef, where carcasses tolled the big fish in. The station is closed now, but large Queensland whites still frequent the area from Brisbane north to Cape Melville, and Brisbane remains an Australian sportfishing center with massive tiger sharks, hammerheads, makos, and blue sharks, as well as the whites. Queensland and New South Wales rank highest in sharking activity, holding most of the country's angler population and tackle shops.

The east coast is affected by the east Australian current, running north to south, and by the south equatorial current. South of Brisbane, the continental slope swings closer to shore, running along the southern portions of Queensland and the entire coast of New South Wales. This is prime tiger and mako country. The season runs year-round although the prime months are from November to April; and the top ports are Swansea, Lake Macquarie, Port Stephens, and Port Hacking.

Port Stephens to Cape Howe

Peter Goadby, one of Australia's top anglers, comments on light-tackle fishing for tigers in the area, "Each weekend at Port Stephens and Lake Macquarie (on the northern coast of New South Wales) and some other ports, tigers in excess of 300 kg (660 pounds) are regularly weighed in on 15-kg (30-lb) tackle." Most of the angling is carried out at the edge of the continental slope; and huge makos, some over 600 pounds, are also taken from these waters.

For tigers, Goadby recommends deep baits, set at depths of 100 to 120 feet, plus inside offerings positioned at 30 feet. Many large tigers and makos will run the slick up to the boat and Peter states that "The best take and hookups come with small baits if they are to be given right at boatside." How big do they get? The largest 30-lb-test tiger on record, at 1,364 pounds, was taken out of Swansea in 1990 by Glen Kirkwood.

For light-tackle makos, Port Stephens ranks high, and both IGFA 30-lb records are held from that port. The largest catch by a woman, at 628 pounds, was taken by Katherine James. The men's 30-lb-class record is held by Robert Gleghorn for a mako which tipped the scales at 936 pounds. Peak seasons run from October to November and February to March.

New South Wales also has excellent blue-shark and hammerhead angling. Blue sharking is best from September to November, and the hammerheads arrive a little later—December through February. The blues run big, often in excess of 400 pounds; and the largest record hammerhead, at 523 pounds, was caught outside of Port Macquarie by Jason Pickles. Local anglers also favor 30-lb-class tackle for these fish, making New South Wales the top spot on the globe for the big-fish/light-tackle brigade.

Australia's continental slope passes the southern end of New South Wales and continues down to the east coast of Tasmania. As a sharking area, this is new ground and may hold future prizes. West of Cape Howe, Victoria contains shallower waters that extend to the sparsely populated South

Zane Grey, the original international angler, with "grey nurse sharks, man-eaters, 300 to 500 pounds," caught at "Batewana Bay," Australia, in 1936.

Australia region. And much of the island continent's Southwest and Northwest is virtually untouched, due to a lack of angling pressure, not to a scarcity of sharks.

New Zealand

New Zealand is ideal for both heavy-and light-tackle sharking: as the original great mako hot spot, the region continues to produce quality mackerel sharking; and its thresher and tope fishery is superb—perhaps the best in the world. Most of the angling is confined to the North Island, along the east coast from Napier northward; and top areas include Hawke Bay, the Bay of Plenty, the Bay of Islands, and Parengarenga

Harbor on the northern frontier.

One of New Zealand's largest makos, a strapping 1,022-pound fish, was taken in Hawke Bay in 1990 by Martin Shanaghan fishing out of Napier. This is relatively new ground, and more fish will come from Hawke in the future.

The Bay of Plenty

The Bay of Plenty, north of Hawke, produces consistent angling from Whakatane at its central shore and from Tauranga on the western side. Outstanding thresher angling is found around Mayor Island off the northwestern shore, accessible by boat from Tauranga. Bay of Plenty waters start to

Brian McGrath Collection

W. W. Dowding's huge 1937 Otehei Bay thresher eclipses the modern all-tackle record by well over 100 pounds and remains one of the greatest shark catches in history.

Pollock, who runs his charter boat *Pursuit* out of Whakatane, runs overnight trips to the White Island grounds. "We catch a number of makos and threshers in the course of the year and have made some captures of large fish." Rick's summertime excursions take advantage of the abundant bait schools of kahawai and the peak times of day—the dusk and dawn "bites," when sharks are often active.

From Tauranga and Tutukaka, the offshore northern Bay of Plenty marks produce sizable makos. It was out of Tutukaka that Joy Clements caught her 697-pound mako, the mark to break on 50-lb-class tackle. Mayor Island is synonymous with threshers and famous for large fish. And at present, Tutukaka and Mayor Island hold four of the heavyweight world records for threshers, the largest being an 802-pound bigeye taken by Dianne North, the apex of modern landings in 1981 and still the all-tackle IGFA record for the species.

We rank the northwestern Bay of Plenty as the top thresher spot in the world. Most local fishermen bait these fish with fresh kahawai, using them live if possible. The New Zealand threshers and makos are also hooked by trolling. A hungry thresher repeatedly slapping the bait is a fascinating sight, and most hookups are followed by acrobatics from these aerialist species.

The Historic Bay of Islands

Farther north along the east coast, we reach New Zealand's historic Bay of Islands. The area first came to world attention in the early part of this century, when the Bay was the premier destination for early British big-game anglers, such as C. Alma Baker, H. White-Wickham, and Lady Broughton.

warm in late December, and January through April are the peak months for threshers and makos.

Since the ban on foreign longlining, the North Island's fisheries have improved; perhaps someday they will again achieve their former angling glory. As a shallow port, Whakatane is a good place for tope, but it offers good blue sharking too. The angling for these two species will delight light-tackle buffs.

White Island, about a 30-mile run out of Whakatane, holds the larger mackerel sharks and threshers that feed on the multitudes of baitfish in the area. Captain Rick

They were after not only broadbill sword-fish and marlin but also the legendary makos which established the species as one of the greatest of all finned game. We believe that the first recorded mako shark was landed here in 1915, second only to C. F. Holder's "bonito shark" in antiquity.

The Bay of Islands also produced another original—a narrow sliver of a craft, the *Alma G.,* which had gained a splendid reputation before Zane Grey fished aboard her early in 1926. As a launch, the *Alma G.* was one of the smaller boats fishing in the Bay. With about 7 feet of beam at the stern and "though the best craft in Russell," Grey first described her as "uncomfortable." After encountering a gale, he revised his thinking: "The *Alma G.* proved a sea-worthy craft and gave me confidence."

A cross between a V-bottomed and round-bottomed craft, the boat was fitted with an oak swivel chair mounted on a stanchion. With Captain Francis Arlidge at the helm and former whaler Peter Williams as cockpit man, the *Alma G.* cruised into history, successfully live-baiting a number of makos on Zane Grey's behalf, including a 702-pound bruiser.

A decade later, Arlidge's boat was still fishing on the North Island when British angler W. W. Dowding caught his incredible world-record thresher—922 pounds. Dowding was so excited that he spent a small fortune cabling the news to his London friends. One laconic associate wired the following message in return: "Put it back!"

Derrydale Press

The Alma G. *when she was younger, with Zane Grey's 702-pound Bay of Islands mako. "This is the brute that came alive and took possession of the cockpit," said Grey (sitting safely on cabin-top).*

Of the hundreds of sharks taken by the *Alma G.,* Dowding's 1937 thresher is still the largest of that species caught on rod and reel. The boat continued fishing for another 50 years, racking up a phenomenal aggregate catch. A couple of years ago, the veteran craft was restored by her then owner, Bob Douch of Paihia, who sold the boat once it was returned to pristine condition. The *Alma G.* survives today and bears witness to the days of wooden rods and iron men.

This rural area still yields the sharks that made it famous, and the town of Russell remains one of the few ports accessing the area. The grounds around Urupukapuka Island, where Grey took 17 makos, produce the same species for modern anglers, the largest local catch being just over a grand. These waters also maintain a solid population of threshers from February, the best month, to June.

Two current line-class-record threshers are from the Bay of Islands; the biggest is a 767-pounder taken in 1983 by D. L. Hannah. The fish is also the third largest of the species ever landed, Dowding's catch included. If we could go anywhere on earth to angle for any fish, we would journey to the Bay of Islands and bait one of its super threshers—from the cockpit of the *Alma G.*

The Tope of Parengarenga Harbor

In closing, we would like to mention the amazing catches at Parengarenga Harbor, in New Zealand's Far North. One look at the IGFA standings shows that this remote area holds no less than 15 class records for tope, including a fish of almost 73 pounds as the all-tackle mark, caught by a talented youngster. As perhaps the last wilderness harbor in temperate seas, Parengarenga hosts one of the few remaining strong runs of the species.

One of Northland's leading light-tackle and conservation exponents, Mark Feldman has also made shark fishing a family tradition. The all-tackle tope, at 72 pounds, 12 ounces, was taken by Melanie Feldman at the age of 6 years. The women's 2-lb-line-class fish, at 36 pounds, 6 ounces, is under Elizabeth M. Feldman's belt, so to speak.

The prime time for tope angling is from early December until February. Parengarenga Harbor is shallow and notorious for shifting sandbars but allows access for a skiff or dinghy. Some of the better tope marks are found in the main channel and down the South Arm, and fish can be found in depths up to 60 feet. Like other skinny-water areas along the North Island, the harbor sees large schools of gravid female tope arrive in early spring. They remain for almost 12 weeks and then depart to cooler waters with the heat of summer.

This is also the period when these fish are vulnerable to commercial gillnets and longlines. According to Mark, these sexually mature fish are harvested with little regard to the damage done. "The commercial fishermen are operating under the illusion that there are lots of school sharks. What they don't realize is that these tope have been concentrating from all over the sea for a once-a-year migration into shallow-water zones." At present the commercial fishermen may see a mandatory 25-percent reduction in their quota, but many Kiwis believe this stopper may not be high enough to reverse the reduction in numbers.

Presently, local anglers are releasing most of these fish, retaining a few for eating and for records. As New Zealand's

Mark Feldman

The current IGFA all-tackle-record tope, at almost
73 pounds. This exceptional New Zealand catch
was made by Melanie Feldman
when she was six years old.

windswept hot spot for large tope, Parengarenga joins the Bay of Plenty and the Bay of Islands to make the North Island one of the very best locations for taking three of the most active shark species.

Regions like Parengarenga Harbor in New Zealand, Australia's New South Wales, the north coast of Scotland, the waters off California, and the Gulf of Maine have the potential to produce great shark angling for generations to come. Our hope is that conservation and release will enable this potential to be realized. Like us, many species of sharks are international, although they don't carry passports or even green cards. When they pass through your local waters, treat them with the respect any international visitor deserves. And they may come back again.

U.S. East Coast Shark Grounds

The following table is compiled from regional data supplied by our contributors and, from *Salt Water Sportsman* magazine: Ray Hendrickson, July 1992; Eric B. Burnley, November 1991; Dick Mermon, November 1991; Joel Arrington, May 1990, January 1991, and February 1992; Donald Millus, December 1991; Captain Doug Kelly, August 1991; and Captain "Marathon John" Cacciutti, February 1992.

Location	Distance (miles)	Depth (feet)	Degrees (magnetic)	Loran-C Readings
From Boothbay Harbor, Maine				
Monhegan SSW	15	280	•	12948/25835
The Wall	7	127–280	ESE	13000/25867
Inner Kettle	16	270–450	210	13100/25885
Outer Kettle	20	300–450	210	13160/25860
From the Saco River, Maine				
Wood Island Ground	4	•	•	13385.7/25992.4
The Gulch	20	•	E	13245/25860
Portland LNB	•	•	•	13285.8/25956.2
The Shark Grounds	25	•	SSE	13290/25810
From Portsmouth, New Hampshire				
Boone Island Ledge	•	•	•	13555.4/25914.7
The Flags	9–10	•	SE	•

Location	Distance (miles)	Depth (feet)	Degrees (magnetic)	Loran-C Readings
From Eastern Point, Cape Ann, Massachusetts				
Stellwagen Bank	20–25	•	SE	•
Wildcat Knoll	•	•	•	13620/25520
Old Man's Pasture	•	•	•	13795/25740
From Block Island, Rhode Island				
Block Island Grounds	15–25	•	SE-SW	•
From Shinnecock Inlet, Long Island, New York				
Butterfish Hole	35–45	120	•	•
The Fish Tales	72	•	146	•
Forty Fath Fingers	40–50	145–170	•	26577/42650
The Dip	66	•	162	•
Hudson Canyon	75	•	190	•
Coimbre Wreck	•	•	•	26203.6/43576.4
From Mannisquam Inlet, New Jersey				
The Mud Hole	20	180	•	•
Monster Ledge	•	•	•	26734/43479
Triple Wrecks	•	•	•	26453/43168
Texas Tower	•	•	•	26313/43268
Bacardi Wreck	•	•	•	26308/43310.6
Oley's Lump	•	•	•	26740/43265
From Mid Jersey Ports				
A.C. Ridge	•	•	•	26867/42902
28-Mile Wreck	•	•	•	26825/42802
750 Squared	•	•	•	26750/42750
30-Fath Lump	•	•	•	26649/42574
From South Jersey Inlets				
Elephant Trunk	•	•	•	26787/42540
Second Dumpsite	•	•	•	26800/42400
19-Fath Lump	•	•	•	26850/42460
Hot Dog	•	•	•	26815/42225
Indian Arrow	•	•	•	26691/42524

Location	Distance (miles)	Depth (feet)	Degrees (magnetic)	Loran-C Readings
From Wachapreague, Virginia				
26 Mile Hill	•	•	•	27000/41580
21 Mile Hill	•	•	•	27020/41700
20 Fath Finger	•	•	•	26930/41700
Parramore Bank	•	•	•	27120/41740
From Rudee Inlet, Virginia				
The Tower	13	•	078	27100.4/41289
Tiger Wreck	10.3	•	119	27101.6/41189
Fish Hook	•	•	•	27045/41240
Hot Dog	•	•	•	26980/41230
Santore Wreck	10	•	072	
4A Buoy Drydock	18	•	149	
From Beaufort Inlet, North Carolina				
Hardee's	24	•	153	27039.3/39575
Carteret	22.5	•	184	27081/39490
Big Rock	•	135–210	•	27085/39575
Atlas	•	130	•	27034.6/39721.6
Amagansett	•	130	•	27027/39724.3
The Papoose	•	130	•	27074/39431.1
U-352	•	115	•	27036.5/39491.8
USS Schurz	•	110	•	27067.6/39463.4
From Masonboro Inlet, North Carolina				
18-Mile Rock	18	•	088	27221.7/39215.9
23-Mile Rock	23.6	•	122	27190/39153.7
Frying Pan Tower	42.0	•	172	27190/39025
Atton Lennon	17.8	•	143	27217.7/39082.9
From Carolina Beach Inlet, North Carolina				
Peteroff Wreck	11.5	•	174	27257.1/57504.6
Grainger Wreck	33.5	•	113	27160/39175.01
WR2 (Cassimer)	42.5	•	106	27128.5/39249.6
From Georgetown Inlet, South Carolina				
Long Bay Terrace	•	90	•	45290/59588
The Horseshoe	•	87	•	45282.6/59871.7

Location	Distance (miles)	Depth (feet)	Degrees (magnetic)	Loran-C Readings
From Georgetown Inlet, South Carolina, cont.				
Santee Banks	•	90	•	45226.4/59913.7
Winyah Scrap	•	600	•	45145/59720
Georgetown Hole	•	570	•	45138/59980
From Fort Lauderdale Inlet, Florida				
Caicos Express	•	265	•	14262.7/62108.7
Corey 'n' Chris	•	244	•	14274.2/62093.4
Lowrance	•	180–220	•	14272.8/62095.3
Mako Reef	•	240	•	14272.0/62096.2
Renegade	•	220	•	14273.4/62094.6
Te Amo	•	215	•	14261.8/62106.6
From the Miami River, Florida				
Tenneco Reef	•	185–190	•	14247.2/62120.8
Cruz Del Sur	•	240	•	14246.1/62121.0
Ultra Freeze	•	120	•	14211.1/62150.0
Sir Scott	•	220	•	14201.2/62157.5
Mystic Isle	•	185	•	14219.4/62142.2
Star Trek	•	210	•	14219.0/62142.2
Lotus	•	216	•	14233.0/43100.1
From The Middle Keys, Florida				
Marathon Hump	•	500	•	14032.5/43358.6
Islamorada Hump	•	498	•	14098.5/43266.5

Depth Equivalents in Feet, Fathoms, and Meters

Feet	•	Fathoms	•	Meters
1	•	0.1667	•	0.3048
3	•	0.5	•	0.9144
3.28	•	0.5467	•	1
6	•	1	•	1.8288
32.8	•	5.467	•	10
60	•	10	•	18.288
65.6	•	10.935	•	20
98.4	•	16.4	•	30
120	•	20	•	36.576
131.2	•	21.871	•	40
164	•	27.338	•	50
180	•	30	•	54.864
196.8	•	32.8	•	60
229.6	•	38.274	•	70
240	•	40	•	73.152
262.4	•	43.742	•	80

Feet	•	Fathoms	•	Meters
295.2	•	49.2	•	90
300	•	50	•	91.44
328	•	54.67	•	100
360	•	60	•	109.728
360.8	•	60.145	•	110
393.6	•	65.613	•	120
420	•	70	•	128.016
426.4	•	71	•	130
459.2	•	76.548	•	140
480	•	80	•	146.304
492	•	82	•	150
524.8	•	87.484	•	160
540	•	90	•	164.592
557.6	•	92.951	•	170
590.4	•	98.419	•	180
600	•	100	•	182.88

F. Y. I.

For information on World Records and Membership:
The International Game Fish Association
1301 East Atlantic Boulevard
Pompano Beach, FL 33060

For information on British Records and Membership:
Sportfishing Club of the British Isles
79 Greenbay Road, Charlton
London SE7 8PX
England, U.K.

For tagging information and "The Shark Tagger" in the United States:
National Marine Fisheries Service
28 Tarzwell Drive
Narragansett, RI 02882-1199

For fishery and tagging information in New Zealand:
Ministry of Agriculture and Fisheries
P.O. Box 207
295 Evans Bay Parade
Wellington, New Zealand

About Our Contributors

From the United States

Captain Barry Gibson is the senior skipper in Boothbay Harbor, Maine, and the editor of *Salt Water Sportsman* magazine. His present boat, the *Shark IV*, is a Down East–style 36-footer, which took a very nice mako during one of her first trips.

Captain Matt Wilder operates the Bertram 35 *Lucky Star II* from the same port and is a well-known East Coast delivery skipper. He has been sharking since 1984.

Captain Cal Robinson is Maine's top sharking and tuna authority and runs Saco Bay Tackle. He has initiated hundreds of new sharkers into the sport.

Kurt Christensen lives in Sebago, Maine, and is an avid sharker. He took one of the recent Gulf of Maine threshers.

Captain Ben Garfield has fished the Gulf of Maine for a decade, successfully operating several charter boats to the shark grounds.

Carl D. Walsh works for Maine's *Biddeford Journal* and is a freelance photojournalist.

Captain Al Ristori is a charter skipper and freelance writer-photographer, who first fished from Montauk, Long Island, and now fishes from Mannisquam, New Jersey. He has taken several hefty makos through the years.

Captain Berle Wilson charters the *Good Times* out of Hatteras Inlet, North Carolina, and specializes in marlin and shark fishing.

Wayne McNamee and Rick West are commercial shark fishermen from North Carolina's Frisco area. They know where the sharks are.

Mark Sosin, from Boca Raton, Florida, is one of sportfishing's most notable angler-writers, a video journalist, and the host of *Salt Water Journal*.

John E. Phillips lives in Fairfield, Alabama, and does freelance writing and photography on fishing in the Gulf of Mexico region.

Larry Bozka is a well-known angler and writer from the Port O'Connor, Texas, area. He is an avid Gulf Coast surf fisherman.

Captain Mike "The Beak" Hurt is a well-respected Southern California skipper, specializing in billfish and sharks. He is also a photographer and a freelance writer.

Abe Cuanang is a long-time freelance writer and angler from San Francisco, California. Abe enjoys bottom-bumping and fly-fishing for blue sharks in local waters and marlin fishing at Cabo San Lucas.

Dave Elm has helped pioneer new methods of taking threshers from his home waters of Southern California. He works for Aftco in Irvine.

From Costa Rica, Great Britain, Australia, and New Zealand

Ray Barry runs the deluxe Silver King Lodge at Barra Colorado on the Caribbean side of Costa Rica, and he's an ardent light-tackle angler.

David John Sneath is publicity officer for the Sportfishing Club of the British Isles and editor of *British Sportfisherman* magazine—when he's not angling.

Captain Ted Legg is one of Great Britain's top skippers, and has developed new live-baiting techniques for aggressive sharks. His boat, the *Kittywake*, holds the European all-tackle thresher record.

Chris Sinclair fishes the waters of western England, specializing in mackerel sharks and tope.

Simon Williams hails from the Caernarvon Bay area of Wales and has avidly fished for tope for the past decade.

Stan Massey is a founding member of the Big Game Club of Scotland and an itinerant porbeagle angler.

Rob Richardson and Chris Bennett are Scottish anglers who also have the distinction of being world-record holders. They are both porbeagle buffs.

Peter Goadby is one of Australia's finest anglers and a well-known author. He specializes in big fish—the marlin, tuna, and monster sharks.

Dr. Mark Feldman is an expert tope angler from New Zealand's North Island and a world-record holder. During the summer he and his family live in Hudson, New Hampshire.

Captain Rick Pollock operates the overnight party boat *Pursuit* out of the Bay of Plenty, New Zealand, and is an avid grouper and shark skipper.

INDEX